FIRST EDITION

THE SOCIAL WORK PRACTITIONER

AN INTRODUCTION TO FUNDAMENTALS OF THE SOCIAL WORK PROFESSION

BY ALLISON SINANAN

STOCKTON UNIVERSITY

Bassim Hamadeh, CEO and Publisher
Kassie Graves, Director of Acquisitions and Sales
Jamie Giganti, Senior Managing Editor
Miguel Macias, Senior Graphic Designer
John Remington, Senior Field Acquisitions Editor
Gem Rabanera, Project Editor
Alexa Lucido, Licensing Coordinator
Abbey Hastings, Associate Production Editor
Joyce Lue, Interior Designer

Cover image copyright © 2016 iStockphoto LP/Steve Debenport.

Printed in the United States of America.

ISBN: 978-1-5165-0133-5 (pbk) / 978-1-5165-0134-2 (br)

 cognella® | ACADEMIC PUBLISHING

CONTENTS

LOCATION OF CURRICULUM CONTENT ASSOCIATED WITH 2015 EPAS COMPETENCY PRACTICE BEHAVIORS: INTRODUCTION TO SOCIAL WORK

COMPETENCIES	PRACTICE BEHAVIORS	COURSE UNIT OF CONTENT
Competency 1– Demonstrate Ethical and Professional Behavior	Make ethical decisions by applying the standards of the NASW Code of Ethics, relevant laws and regulations, models for ethical decision-making, ethical conduct of research, and additional codes of ethics as appropriate to context; use reflection and self-regulation to manage personal values and maintain professionalism in practice situations;	**Part 1: THE SOCIAL WORK PROFESSION** 1. Definition of Social Work and Key Concepts 2. History of the Social Work Profession
Competency 2 – Engage Diversity and Difference in Practice	apply and communicate understanding of the importance of diversity and difference in shaping life experiences in practice at the micro and macro levels; present themselves as learners and engage clients and constituencies as experts of their own experiences; Apply self-awareness and self-regulation to manage the influence of personal biases and values in working with diverse clients and constituencies.	**Part 3: CULTURAL COMPETENCE: WORKING WITH OPPRESSED POPULATIONS** 5. What is Cultural Competence and Why is it Important? 6. At-Risk Communities: Examining Poverty
Competency 3 – Advance Human Rights and Social, Economic, and Environmental Justice	Engage in practices that advance social, economic, and environmental justice.	**Part 2: SOCIAL WORK PRACTICE** 3. Social Work Generalist Practice 4. Values and Code of Ethics in Social Work Practice
Competency 6- Engage with individuals, families, groups, organizations, and communities.	Use empathy, reflection, and interpersonal skills to effectively engage diverse clients and constituencies.	**Part 4: SERVING VARIOUS CLIENT POPULATIONS** 7. Practice Settings and Fields of Social Work 8. Working with Individuals 9. Working with Groups and Communities 10. Social Work Practice with Organizations and Communities 11. Practice Settings for Social Workers: Providing Social Work Services for Children and Families or Older Adults 12. Providing Social Work Services in a Variety of Settings with Different Populations 13. Social Work Today & The Future of the Profession

PART 1

THE SOCIAL WORK PROFESSION

1

DEFINITION OF SOCIAL WORK AND KEY CONCEPTS OF THE PROFESSION

LEARNING OBJECTIVES

After reading this chapter, one should be able to

- provide a definition of social work, and
- identify the values of the profession.

A LOOK INTO THE SOCIAL WORK PROFESSION

Social work is a helping profession with an extensive scope of concern; a profession that has core values with a robust pledge to ensure, and working towards, social and economic justice for all members of society. What makes social work different than other helping professions is the perspective of seeing the client in his or her environment and recognizing that there are external factors that play a part in the client's presenting issue. Professionals in this field take a comprehensive view, a view that looks at the client's social environment, including the their family, home, work, health, community, friends and the interactions between these systems. This chapter provides an overview of what social workers do and examines some of the core skills and values used in the profession.

DEFINITION OF SOCIAL WORK

Social work's mission is to promote economic and social justice, and to work against the hindrance of circumstances and situations that limit human rights, by supporting the enhancement of the quality of life for all individuals (Council on Social Work Education, Educational Policy and Accreditation Standards, 2015). The social worker engages at the points where people interact with their environments. Philosophies of human rights & social justice are central factors to social work (International Federation of Social Workers, 2000).

SO WHY DOES ONE CHOOSE TO ENTER THE PROFESSION?

Many social workers have stated that at an early age, they constantly helped others and enjoyed being part of a support system for those who needed them. Another common theme of professionals in the field is that many social workers feel that their family members and friends always came to them for help or to act as a listening ear. Have any interest in helping others? Want to make a real difference? Are you searching for a career that is fulfilling yet challenging? If these questions are common in your thoughts when thinking about which career to pursue, then perhaps this textbook can shed some light on answers to some of these questions for you. Social work is a rewarding, hands-on career that makes a difference, whether on an individual, group or community level. The majority of those who enter the field earn an undergraduate degree in social work before entering graduate school; some other undergraduate majors, such as psychology, pursue a social work master's program after receiving their degrees.

BASIC GOALS OF SOCIAL WORK

Social work is unique among other helping disciplines because of its broad scope of concern, its strong core values, and its commitment to social and economic justice. The social work profession realizes how the environment and certain circumstance can and may significantly impact the social functioning of individuals, groups, and communities. One of the main goals of the profession includes enhancing the client's social functioning and to assist in creating a more unbiased and supportive society. Social work, an applied practice, is a professional and academic discipline, with a specified body of values, knowledge, and skills that incorporates a perspective that looks at the individual as a whole. Professionals in the field do not view presenting problems as personal pathology, but rather, recognizes that the environment, lack of resources, society, as well as other systemic factors, play a part in the client's presenting issue.

Social work is the professional action of helping individuals, groups, or communities to restore or enhance their capacity for social functioning and to produce societal conditions favorable to their clients' goals (National Association of Social Workers [NASW], 1973). The social work profession promotes social change, the empowerment and liberation of people, problem solving in human relationships, and improves well-being. Theories of human behavior, social systems, and social theories are utilized to understand and realize how human problems impact the individual, to help improve people's lives, and improve society as a whole.

Social workers work with all individuals in all segments of society, ranging from different socio-economic classes, with various mental and physical health issues, age ranges, and races. Social workers aid individuals to increase their abilities to problem solve and cope. This includes helping clients obtain needed resources and improving interactions between people and their environments. Social workers can work directly with clients in a variety of ways including: 1) working on individual, family, and community issues; 2) working on regulations and policy development at a systems level; 3) or working as administrators of large social service agencies (Barker, 2003). Social workers assist clients with a whole array of issues, including interpersonal, mental or physical health, behavioral, and substance abuse problems to name a few. The professional activities that social workers are trained in involve the following:

- conducting needs assessments;
- providing information and referrals;
- accessing resources in social casework and case management;
- serving as case managers and counseling for specific health-related issues in medical social work;
- working with students and their families on emotional, social, and economic concerns to enable the social worker to focus on the student's education is school social work;
- counseling individuals, families, and groups in such settings as hospitals, schools, mental health facilities, and private practices in clinical social work;
- supervising programs and people in administration and management;
- working to influence the development, implementation, and evaluation of policies aimed at creating social justice for those impacted by policies in policy practice groups and communities;
- working with groups and communities to identify adverse conditions and develop strategies to address them in community organizations; and
- analyzing conditions, programs, and policies and conducting and studying research in an effort to improve the social service system in social policy research.

NATIONAL ASSOCIATION OF SOCIAL WORKERS (NASW)

The National Association of Social Workers (NASW) is the biggest membership organization of professional social workers, with over 132,000 members; it was established in 1955. The

NASW has a chapter in every state in the United States; major cities such as Washington, D.C., New York City, and Puerto Rico have their own chapters, and there is also an International Chapter. NASW's key tasks include creating and maintaining professional standards of social work practice, advancing social policies, upholding the professional development of its members, and providing services that protect its members and enhance their professional status. It developed the *NASW Code of Ethics* which is proposed as a guide for the professional conduct of social workers.

The NASW definition of social work includes four basic goals: (1) connecting individuals to resources; (2) offering direct services to individuals, families, groups, or communities; (3) aiding communities or groups by improving social and health services; and (4) being active in legislative processes relevant to the populations the profession serves (NASW, 1973). The profession is dedicated to social and economic justice and the well-being of marginalized and oppressed individuals and communities, combating racism, classism, heterosexism, sexism, adultism, mentalism, ableism and ageism.

The following section examines the core values that the profession implements to better assist client populations (e.g., client empowerment, self-determination, planned change process, strengths based approach, and person in environment).

CLIENT EMPOWERMENT

Social workers aid in empowering clients by providing them with knowledge and skills. Empowerment is an interactive process that occurs between an individual and their environment. In essence, the sense of self as insignificant transforms into an acceptance of the self, and hence increases the belief in ability for positive change. This consciousness enables the ability to participate with others, to deal and cope with frustrations, and to recognize one's influence over the environment (Kieffer, 1984). A strengths based approach aids with client empowerment; it provides the social worker with a theoretical basis for empowering the client. This approach helps boost self-awareness and self-esteem in an effort to increase a sense of power, leading to a desired outcome. Empowerment is both a process and an outcome.

STRENGTHS-BASED APPROACH

Strengths-based approach is a social work practice theory that emphasizes people's strengths. With this approach, the professional views clients as resourceful beings with a capacity for resilience when faced with adversity (Healy, 2005). This is contrary to the medical, or deficit model, in which a practitioner focuses on what may be wrong with the individual, and are inclined to solely focus on the problem as opposed to recognizing the client's strengths to bring about change.

Social workers begin with a focus on client strengths for many reasons. Often in our society, as in most, people have a tendency to focus on problems and on what is going wrong without looking at the resources at their disposal; some may find it hard to identify strengths within themselves. A core job of the social worker is to help the client see their strengths and identify ways to utilize these strengths to bring about positive change. This change can be changes in behavior, in thinking, or actual concrete changes. This initial process of identifying strengths can help build client self-esteem and strengthen family relationships. Identifying one's strengths aids in instilling hope and provides motivation for change.

SELF-DETERMINATION

Self-determination is a component of client empowerment that concentrates on allowing clients to be presented with all options available in order to make the most informed decisions. Self-determination is a key value of the profession because it embraces the belief that the client is an expert in his/her life, capable of independently making choices and decisions. The social worker guides, educates, and supports the client in this process. According to NASW, social workers promote and respect clients' right to self-determination and helps clients recognize and clarify their goals. At specific times, social workers' professional judgment may lead them to limit a client's right to self-determination if the clients' actions or future actions pose a severe, foreseeable, and imminent risk to themselves or others (e.g., if the client is suicidal, a danger to others, or a perpetrator of child abuse; NASW 2015).

PLANNED CHANGE PROCESS

When working with clients, social workers use a series of steps to aid clients in resolving their presenting problems. These steps are referred to as the *planned change process*. The planned change process includes four phases: engagement, assessment, intervention, and evaluation. The first step, the engagement phase, involves getting to know the client, establishing trust and building a relationship (rapport), and laying the groundwork for collaboration. During the second step, the assessment phase, the social worker and client recognize and identify the problem(s). The social worker may need to determine the level of risk of client harm to self or others. The third stage, the intervention stage, involves planning and implementing interventions with the client; they establish measurable goals and identify steps to meet those goals. The last phase of the process, evaluation, involves gathering baseline data and benchmark data along the way to determine progress toward the client reaching the stated goals. In every activity a social worker is involved in, evaluation is a key component to inform the social worker, and sometimes the profession as a whole, if the interventions are making a difference and doing what they are supposed to being doing.

PERSON-IN-ENVIRONMENT

The person-in-environment perspective has been acknowledged by the profession as distinctively differentiating social work from related professions, such as psychology (person centered) and sociology (more organizationally oriented). The person-in-environment perspective is a practice-guiding principle that emphasizes the significance of viewing a person in the context of the environmental factors that are present and can or may impact a client. When assessing problems and planning interventions, social workers take into account the environmental factors contributing to the problem. Social workers believe that unhealthy environments contribute to unhealthy development of relationships, skills, attitudes, and beliefs. Florence Hollis originally coined the phrase person-in-environment (PIE) in 1964. (Hollis, 1964).

LEVELS OF INTERVENTION

Social work is an academic and professional discipline that aims to improve and enhance the quality of life and of individuals, couples, families, groups, and communities. Social work professionals work with people in all segments of society, from those who are disenfranchised or devalued by society and living in poverty, to those in the middle and upper socioeconomic segments of the population. They work with the young and old, people in good and poor health, and from diverse cultures and backgrounds. Action occurs through direct practice, policy planning, research, crisis intervention, and community development to ensure social welfare and security for those impacted by societal disadvantages like poverty, provide psychosocial care to physically and mentally disabled individuals, prevent maltreatment of children, and raise awareness against social injustice and for social reforms. Therefore, social workers intervene at three levels: micro, mezzo, and macro, by providing support to individuals, families, groups, organizations and communities.

The profession has four basic goals: (a) linking people to resources; (b) providing direct services to individuals, families, and groups; (c) being involved in relevant legislative processes; (d) assisting communities or groups to or enhance social and health services. These roles are not exclusive, and an average day on the job may very well include multiple roles. Some of the many roles of social workers include: initiator, activist, group facilitator, advocate, educator, case manager, enabler, broker, counselor, mediator, and evaluator.

ROLES OF SOCIAL WORKERS

Macro Practice Settings

- Community organization: works with governmental, private, civic, religious, business, and trade organizations to address social problems

- Social policy research: analyzes conditions, programs, and policies and conducts and studies research in an effort to improve the social service system
- Administration: supervises programs and people
- Initiator: Recognizes and calls attention to a problem
- Activist: Takes action for change on behalf of others to promote social justice
- Group Facilitator: Takes a leadership role within task and treatment groups
- Advocate: Promotes the client's position or need
- Mobilizer: Organizes and empowers community members to achieve goals
- Educator: Provides information and teaches skills
- Case Manager: Coordinates the services and resources of multiple agencies
- Enabler: Helps clients build the capacity to deal with challenges
- Counselor: Helps clients identify problems and intervention strategies
- Broker: Links clients with needed resources
- Mediator: Serves in a dispute resolution mode between two parties
- Evaluator: Collects data to determine the effectiveness of interventions

SOCIAL WORK EDUCATION

The NASW asserts that only those individuals holding degrees in social work should be referred to as "social workers"; many states have adopted this law or policy. This requirement guards the field from having individuals employed as "social workers" without degrees in social work; i.e., a bachelor's or master's degree from a university or college accredited by the Council on Social Work Education (CSWE). Social work licensure assists with standards for the title of "social worker," thereby eliminating unqualified, untrained individuals from the field. The CSWE is the only accrediting agency for schools of social work education in the United States. As of October 2012, there are 479 accredited baccalaureate social work programs and 218 accredited master's social work programs.

CSWE's mission is to encourage and strengthen the quality of social work education by setting policy and program standards, and accrediting bachelor's and master's level social work programs to prepare competent social work professionals.

The following degrees are offered in the field of Social Work:

- Bachelor of Social Work (BSW): A four year degree from an accredited school of social work that prepares the graduate for generalist social work professional practice.
- Master of Social Work (MSW): A two year degree from an accredited school of social work following the completion of a four year degree, which prepares the graduate to work in an advanced professional practice in an area of concentration. If one already has a BSW, then the individual qualifies for advanced standing and can earn an MSW in one year.

- Doctorate in Social Work (PhD or DSW)—A Doctor of Philosophy in Social Work and a Doctorate of Social Work are considered research-oriented degrees with a focus on preparing the graduate for a teaching or research career, or advanced clinical practice.
- Social workers with a master's degree and license may provide psychotherapy. As a result of training, social workers take into account the person-in-environment perspective and look at environmental factors that may be influencing an individual's problems. They are also trained to serve in multiple roles (see Section Six) and look at multiple levels of intervention. Field education provides opportunities for students to apply classroom learning in practice settings under the supervision of highly qualified professionals. Additionally, students are able to test and evaluate their developing competencies as generalist social work practitioners in field as well as integrate their experiences into classroom learning assignments. is an integral part of social work education required by every MSW and BSW program that provides the opportunity to put theory into practice.
- It helps guide students' career directions, narrow their field of practice, observe social work professionals in action, and build self confidence. It also enhances students' resumes, future marketability, and career networks.

LICENSURES IN SOCIAL WORK

LSW—Licensed Social Worker: The requirements for licensure vary by state. Most states require an MSW and an exam. To view the requirements for your state visit the Association of Social Work Boards (ASWB) website.

LCSW—Licensed Clinical Social Worker: These requirements also vary by state. In many states this designation requires an MSW, two years of supervised work in the field, and an exam. The ASWB website describes these requirements. With an LCSW a social worker is eligible for reimbursement for therapy services from insurance companies and may establish a private practice.

WHERE DO SOCIAL WORKERS WORK?

The U.S. Department of Labor documents that five out of every ten social workers work in the health care and social assistance sectors (Bureau of Labor Statistics, 2015). These settings may include mental health clinics, private practices, and hospitals. Thirty percent of all social workers are working in government agencies at the state or local level. Individuals employed in government positions may be involved in child welfare assessments, helping individuals obtain public assistance, and assisting individuals involved in the criminal justice system. Social workers have a wide variety of opportunities to help others in a variety of settings, some of which are listed below:

- justice and corrections,
- child welfare,

- aging,
- research,
- substance misuse and addictions,
- public welfare,
- school social work,
- developmental disabilities,
- health care,
- employment social work,
- clinical and mental health,
- community organization,
- international social work,
- administration and management,
- policy and planning, and
- politics

The most common settings for direct practice social workers are mental health, physical health, and family and children's services. Social workers provide more than 60% of mental health services. Most direct practice social workers engage in additional activities such as administration, supervision, teaching of social work students, and fundraising.

Fig 1.1

Percentage of Social Workers in Different Fields

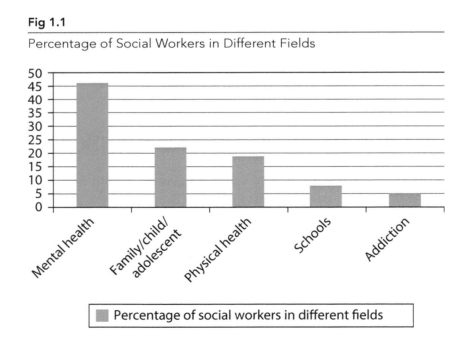

SPECIALTY AREAS IN THE PROFESSION

During the course of many bachelor's and master's degree programs, social workers may choose to specialize in specific fields of practice. Specialization offers social workers more experience and knowledge in their field of interest. Common areas of specialization include clinical, school, child and family social work, gerontology, mental health, and substance abuse.

CLINICAL SOCIAL WORK

Clinical social work, also frequently referred to as a mental health specialization, is usually only available to master's level students; clinical social workers must have a master's degree to practice. Some undergraduate programs may offer a specialization in child welfare, mental health or addictions. Clinical social work specializations may focus on assessment, diagnosis and treatment of mental illness, psychological disorders, and the treatment of relationship and family problems. Clinical social workers are employed in settings such as private practice, mental health clinics, hospitals, and community centers.

SCHOOL SOCIAL WORK

School social workers provide assessments, intervention and counseling to students in an academic setting. This specialization is mainly intended for students who already know that they want to ultimately work in a school. School social workers are usually master's level practitioners, so this specialization is primarily offered in master's degree programs, although some states do not require an MSW, and a BSW will suffice. This track of study offers specific coursework in school social work and field placements in school settings.

CHILD AND FAMILY SOCIAL WORK

Many bachelor's and master's degree programs provide the opportunity to specialize in child and family social work, sometimes referred to as child welfare. At the bachelor's level of practice, child and family social work usually involves working to improve the welfare and safety of children, adolescents, and their families. Typical job settings might include working for a state's child protective services (CPS) agency as a caseworker who makes home visits and investigates allegations of child abuse and neglect. Professionals with a master's degree may specialize in the clinical treatment of children and families in clinical settings providing mental health services, assessments, diagnoses, or individual, family and group therapy to children or families, or both.

SOCIAL WORK AND THE AGING

Social workers who work with the aging or elderly may provide services that include assessments, supportive counseling, advocacy, and concrete services (assistance with eligibility for social programs, housing, etc.). Bachelor's and master's level students interested in working with older adults may select this specializationto gain education and experience needed to work in settings such as home health-care agencies and community centers for older adults.

MENTAL HEALTH AND SUBSTANCE ABUSE

Mental health and substance abuse social workers treat and assess clients suffering from addiction, mental health problems and/or substance abuse problems. Social workers specializing in this area may provide addiction counseling, crisis counseling, individual or group therapy, and psychosocial services.

CHAPTER EXERCISES

1. Identify five activities that social workers are trained for.

2. Identify three key tasks of concern to the NASW.

3. How do the basic goals in the NASW definition of social work distinguish the profession from other helping professions?

4. Name four roles of social workers and provide an example of each role with a specific client population.

5. Name a specialty area of social work that interests you and discuss why you would like to work in that field or with that specific population.

REFERENCES

Bureau of Labor Statistics. (2015). *Occupational Outlook Handbook*. Retrieved from http://www.bls.gov/ooh/community-and-social-service/social-workers.htm

Council on Social Work Education (CSWE). (2015). *2015 Educational Policy and Accreditation Standards (EPAS)*. Retrieved from http://www.cswe.org/File.aspx?id=81660

Healy, K. (2005). *Social work theories in context: Creating frameworks for practice*. New York: Palgrave Macmillan.

Hollis, F. (1964). *Casework: A psychosocial therapy*. New York: Random House.

International Federation of Social Workers. (2000). *International code of ethics for the professional social worker*. Geneva, Switzerland.

Keiffer, C. (1984). Citizen empowerment: A developmental perspective. *Prevention in Human Services, 3* (16), 9–35.

National Association of Social Workers. (1973). *Standards for social service manpower*. Washington, DC: NASW.

National Association of Social Workers . (2015). *Standards for code of ethics*. Retrieved from https://www.naswpress.org/publications/standards/code.htm

2

HISTORY OF THE SOCIAL WORK PROFESSION

LEARNING OBJECTIVES

After reading this chapter, the reader will be able to

- provide a thorough summary of the history of the social work profession,
- identify notable instrumental individuals who helped shape the profession, and
- identify where social work is going in the 21st century.

HISTORY OF THE SOCIAL WORK PROFESSION

Why is the history of a profession important you ask? Knowing the history of this profession is one of the most essential aspects in becoming a social worker. Social workers today must know how the profession started to appreciate all that has been accomplished. In addition, historical knowledge is essential because we are continuously fighting and advocating for some of the same basic goals since the beginning.

The concept of aiding others has been in existence since the beginning of time. Ancient civilizations took care of the sick and poor. The majority of religious teachings emphasize providing assistance to those who are less fortunate. Initially, the Catholic Church and one's family provided assistance, i.e., social services, as we know them today. Government placed responsibility for those in need onto extended families to ensure that children and elderly members received care. Churches were obliged to care for orphans, the poor, and those who were extremely ill. Hence, the roots of the social work profession lie within religious communities. Throughout the Middle Ages, Feudalism was the main structure of society in Europe. Under Feudalism, the lords and nobility had responsibility for the serfs and peasants. In 1563 England starting using a registry at the parishes to ensure individuals who were considered "poor" in an effort to reduce these individuals from attempting to get services from more than one parish.

Due to the increasing number of poor in Great Britain and as the feudal system began to crumble, many individuals who needed services drifted to the cities and larger towns. Due to the influx of individuals in need of services and basic needs (i.e., food and shelter) the Elizabethan Poor Law was enacted. The Elizabethan Poor Law (1601) is considered the first legislation to address the issue of caring for those in need. Poverty became a national problem due to the influx of individuals without sufficient skills to earn a living wage. Finally, the Poor Law of 1601 provided a clear definition of the "poor". This legislation is the foundation for the current social welfare system existing today in Great Britain. The Poor Laws utilized the concept of mandatory taxation to fund social and financial assistance; it represents a clear shift away the private sector to governmental responsibility with respect to social services for the poor. These social services were now provided to individuals deemed eligible for assistance in three categories:

The category of poor was divided into three subcategories:

- the able-bodied or deserving poor—those who would work but could not,
- the idle poor—those who could work but would not, and
- the impotent or deserving poor—those who were too old, ill, or young to work.

Monetary help collected through property taxes was used for those who qualified as *deserving poor* (old, young, and sick) and *deserving unemployed* (willing and able to work but unable to find employment). It is quite obvious that after 400 years later, the United States holds true to the same ideologies. In order to collect assistance, recipients of aid were often obliged to live in a residential institution referred to as a workhouse or poorhouse for adults, and orphanages for children; this was also referred to as *indoor relief*. In the 1900s, outdoor relief was introduced. Indoor relief designated the provision of services in an institution such as a workhouse or asylum

Efforts in 17th century England to restrict access to aid for the poor took the form of the 1662 Law of Settlement, stipulating that aid was to be based on one's place of residence.

The United States, soon after achieving independence, made efforts to create a public social and health service system. The early settlers carried with them the traditions and ideologies of England; hence social services and aid were primarily based on the Elizabethan Poor Laws established in England. When the United States was affected by poverty in the early years, Elizabethan Poor Laws were introduced with the purpose of tackling the threat of poverty.

THE HISTORY OF SOCIAL WELFARE IN THE UNITED STATES

In the early years of the United States, the colonies used the British Poor Laws for establishing laws for aid to the poor. The British Poor Laws made a distinction between individuals who were able-bodied but unemployed and those who were unable to work due to their physical health or age. The latter group was assisted with money or alternative forms of assistance from the government. The former group was provided public service employment in workhouses.

THE 1700s

In 1657, the first social welfare agency was founded in Boston; concurrently, the site of the first almshouse was established in New York. The first orphanage was opened in the French colony of New Orleans in 1729. These new institutions were mostly private and religion based. In Charleston, South Carolina, the first government-funded orphanage was established in 1790. The U.S. Public Health Service, which still operates today, was established in 1798 to provide health services to merchant seamen.

THE 1800s

The Industrial Revolution occurred in the late 1800s and early 1900s, and brought about a migration of the population from rural areas to urban living situations. The new demographics created by the migration led to different challenges in social service delivery. Migrants and immigrants were separated from their extended families, causing a significant loss in familial social support systems. By the end of the 1800s, the economy of the United States had begun shifting from agricultural to industrial due to the influx of immigrants from Europe, particularly the new immigrants resulting in a reduced sense of community as many individuals found themselves living among strangers. At the same time, two new social welfare movements emerged, both of which represented types of outdoor relief: Charity Organization Society and The Settlement House movements.

CHARITY ORGANIZATION SOCIETY

In response to the needs of the urban poor, The Charity Organization Societies (COS) were founded in England in 1869 in an effort to harshly limit outdoor relief distributed by the Poor Law Guardians. Guardian of the poor refers to a person who is in charge of the relief and maintenance of the poor in parish. The Charity Organization Societies were imported from England to the United States in 1877. The Charity Organization Societies were primarily concerned with the distinction between the deserving poor and undeserving poor. The believed that only the deserving poor should be provided with aid. Outdoor relief, the provision of services in the community, was created in an effort to improve poverty without the requirement that the recipient enter an institution (i.e., indoor relief). Aid was provided in the form of money, food, clothing or goods.

The first COS in the United States was established in Buffalo, NY in 1877. The principle ideology of the Charity Organization Societies was that *friendly visiting*, and not free handouts, could help people move out of poverty. A principal belief behind the COS movement was that simply giving out aid without investigating the causes behind poverty created citizens that would always be dependent on aid. Volunteers from these organizations, known as visiting philanthropists, visited the homes of poor individuals to provide education and support and to investigate what circumstances caused their poverty. Typically, these philanthropists were White women from middle-income homes. The COS movement has been criticized for its hypercritical nature of blaming the victim for their circumstances, though the movement does receive credit for forming the basis of casework and family services. Mary Richmond was a noteworthy individual who pioneered the Charity Organization Societies and the social work profession in general.

MARY ELLEN RICHMOND (1861–1928)

Mary Richmond was a remarkable social work practitioner, teacher, and theoretician who created the first inclusive statement of principles of social work practice. Ms. Richmond was born in Belleville, Illinois. At the age of 28, she joined the Baltimore Charity Organization and became the assistant treasurer. In 1891 she was appointed the organization's general secretary. In addition, she volunteered as a friendly visitor (NASW, 2016).

Mary Richmond recognized that there was no systematic method to the work being done by these volunteers. She encouraged the application of scientific principles and a formalized coordination of relief efforts. Her efforts led to the beginnings of professional casework. In 1897 Mary Richmond presented a paper at a national conference on the need for a training school for the visiting philanthropists and the following year, a summer school training workshop was established at Columbia University in New York. This was the first formal training program available for social workers. In 1915, her most renowned book, *Social Diagnosis (1922)*, was grounded in her lectures and on her readings in medical social work, law, history, psychiatry, and psychology. The book was instrumental for the profession because it was the first time anyone had combined theory and method in identifying and treating the issues facing clients. In her 1922 book, *What is Social Casework*, Richmond defined social casework as processes which develop personality through adjustments consciously effected, individual by individual, between men and their social environment. These books helped establish the scientific methodology of social work, provided the beginnings of an outline for the social work profession, and were critical to training social workers.

SETTLEMENT HOUSE MOVEMENT

The Settlement House movement also arose due to the influx of immigrants into the United States, and occurred at the same time as the COS movement. Early settlement houses were focused on serving the growing immigrant population. The settlement house movement started in Britain in 1884, which included middle-class London reformers who established the first settlement house, named Toynbee Hall. Toynbee Hall provided social services and education to the poor workers who lived in East London. Motivated by this British action, American social reformers started creating settlement houses in the late 1880s as to deal with the growing poverty among industrial workers. A settlement house is a facility based in a geographically bound neighborhood whose purpose is to provide a center for the neighbors to come together for educational, social, and cultural activities. The central aim of the settlement house was to aid in assimilation by teaching immigrants middle-class American values to ease their transition into the labor force. Supporters of the settlement house movement believed that social workers must be immersed in their community in order to truly identify the existing social problems.

In 1886 Stanton Coit founded the first US settlement house, named Neighborhood Guild, in New York City. Jane Addams and her friend Ellen Starr founded Hull House, the most famous settlement house in the US, in Chicago in 1889. There were 74 settlement houses in the United States by the year 1887; by 1890 the number increased to over 400. Forty percent of settlement houses were in Chicago, Boston, and New York, but the majority of small cities had at least one settlement house. In Chicago, the Hull House assisted in educating immigrants by providing classes in art, history, and literature. The Hull House also provided social services like a daycare center, a homeless shelter, a public kitchen, and public baths in an effort to decrease the effects of poverty.

African-American churches founded settlement houses to provide social services to Black migrants who were moving from the South into the Northern states. In Chicago, Reverend Reverdy Ransom founded the African Methodist Episcopal Institutional Church to provide employment, education, and welfare services to Black migrants; in an effort to deal with the racism that affected many settlement houses, African-American churches became involved in this movement. Though European immigrants were deemed capable of being assimilated into middle-class American society, African-Americans were not viewed in the same light. This eventually led to segregation of Black settlement houses from White settlement houses.

An important factor to note about the two movements addressing a changing America and poverty is the fact that most of the movements' important leadership roles were filled by women, in an era when women were still excluded from leadership roles in business and government; they did not get the right to vote until 1919! Approximately half of the major US settlement houses were led and staffed predominantly by women. Among the most influential leaders were Jane Addams, Mary Simkhovitch, Helena Dudley, Lillian Wald, Mary McDowell, Florence Kelley, Alice Hamilton, and Edith Abbott.

JANE ADDAMS (1860–1935)

Jane Addams, often referred to as the mother of social work, is well known for her pioneering efforts in the profession. In 1889 she and Ellen Gates Starr co-founded the first settlement house for immigrants in the United State, Hull House in Chicago, Illinois. Hull House provided immigrants with opportunities such as adult education, kindergarten, and arts programs. These Hull Houses integrated a belief system that incorporated the same values upon which social work is based on today: 1) respect for ethnic diversity, 2) viewing everyone with dignity, and 3) recognizing the self-worth of every individual. Unlike the COS, where poverty and lack of a job was viewed as the individual's fault, within the settlement house movement, unemployment was viewed as a lack of opportunity. In 1931 Jane Addams became the first woman to win the Nobel Peace Prize. She continued to live and work at Hull House until her death in 1935. Richmond and Addams were both early advocates of the belief that a person's environment influenced their life situation and of looking at the strengths of an individual. Their ideas in these areas continue to impact social work education and practice (NASW, 1998).

SOCIAL WORK EMERGING AS A PROFESSION: 1900s

The Progressive Era of the early 1900s was a time of reform in areas such as women's rights, health care, social services, education, political practices, occupational and consumer safety, child and social welfare laws, environmental preservation, and immigration. Dr. Richard Cabot was instrumental in providing the social work profession with a place in the hospital setting. In 1905 Dr. Cabot hired a social worker to deliver the first professional social work services ever offered in the outpatient clinics of Massachusetts General Hospital; the first hired social worker was Garnet Pelton (Beder, 2006). Dr. Cabot believed that external factors such as social, economic, family, and psychological conditions contributed to patients' well-being and therefore, there was the value in what the profession could bring. He envisioned social workers in a complementary relationship with doctors, providing assistance and care for the patient's social well-being.

Another prominent individual who made a significant contribution to the care of individuals, specifically those with mental illness, was Dorothea Dix. Dorothea Dix was a social reformer whose passion for the welfare of the mentally ill led to widespread international reforms. After seeing horrendous conditions in a Massachusetts prison, Ms. Dix spent 40 years lobbying U.S. and Canadian legislators to found state hospitals for the mentally ill, leading to the construction of 32 institutions in the United States. After volunteering to teach Sunday school for female inmates, Dorothea Dix found that mentally ill individuals were housed together with criminals in dreadful, unsanitary conditions, including lack of heat. Many social workers are inspired by Dorothea Dix, as an example of someone who truly did make a difference in the lives of so many others.

NATIONAL ASSOCIATION FOR THE ADVANCEMENT OF COLORED PEOPLE (NAACP)

The founding of the NAACP in 1909 was rooted in a response to lynching and racial riots in Springfield, IL (http://www.naacp.org/oldest-and-boldest). /The NAACP, originally named the National Negro Committee, was created to defend the civil and Constitutional rights for all people based on the principle that all people are created equal, primarily through an aggressive watchdog system to eliminate racial bias. In the Midwest during this time, many Whites were annoyed that a substantial number of Blacks were leaving behind the oppression of the South and moving to cities, taking over jobs that Whites held, and prospering.

Membership of the NAACP was initially made up of a mix of powerful and strong-minded individuals. The founding members were a large group of White liberals, including Mary White Ovington, William English Walling, Ida B. Wells, Oswald Garrison Villard, and Henry Moscowitz, and seven Blacks, including W.E.B. Du Bois. In 1911 it became the nonprofit entity we know today (Harris, 1992).

The NAACP's political advocacy has reaped numerous monumental victories, such as the passing of anti-lynching laws in some states and the *Brown vs. Board of Education* case, which made education segregation unlawful. This organization continues to impact issues involving racial and social injustices today. The NAACP addresses the cultural and socioeconomic needs of disadvantaged and underrepresented African Americans and other minority groups.

THE NEW DEAL (1930s)

In 1932, when Franklin D. Roosevelt was elected president, he and Congress enacted the New Deal, a package of programs and regulations designed to help the nearly one-third of Americans living in poverty due to the Great Depression. The New Deal programs focused on the "3 Rs," Relief, Recovery, and Reform: relief for the poor and unemployed, recovery of the economy to standard levels, and reform of the financial system to prevent another depression. Notable outcomes of the New Deal included: the Social Security system, which provided assistance to the elderly and disabled; the Federal Emergency Relief Administration, which created employment for over eight million people; and Aid to Dependent Children (later

AFDC and now TANF, commonly known as "welfare"), which provided income to needy families. Frances Perkins, who had been a volunteer at Hull House, was the first woman appointed to the U.S. Cabinet, serving as the U.S. Secretary of Labor from 1933 to 1945. Perkins assisted with writing a majority of the New Deal legislation, including the development of the Social Security Act of 1935 (Axinn & Stein 2005).

1940s AND 1950s

Social workers developed and administered mental health plans for military personnel during the 1940s leading to the creation of the nationwide, community-based mental health system that remains the basis for the provision of mental health services today. In 1944, Roosevelt signed the GI bill to offer financial assistance to veterans returning from World War II. The GI Bill offered a college education to one million veterans. In 1950 President Truman signed an amendment to the Social Security Act to provide a Cost of Living Adjustment to offset inflation (COLA). The Department of Health, Education, and Welfare was created in 1953 during the administration of Dwight D. Eisenhower (1953–1961).

In 1955 the National Association of Social Workers provided a code of ethics that defines the roles and responsibilities for professionals in the field. Social workers were strong proponents of these social service reforms. Social workers highlighted the psychological impact of unemployment and its effect on an individual's self-respect and self-esteem. They emphasized the importance of providing jobs rather than direct financial support in order to help increase an individual's sense of personal worth.

Throughout the implementation of The New Deal and onward to the Civil Rights movement, social workers continued to be at the forefront of the fight for social justice and the reform of social conditions. According to the preamble of the NASW Code of Ethics, the *"principal charge of the social work profession is to enhance human well-being and aid in meeting the basic human needs and empowerment of individuals who are oppressed, vulnerable, and living in poverty."* It is easy to see how this mission propels social workers toward increasing tolerance, ending discrimination, and becoming involved in the struggle for civil rights (NASW, 1973).

The *Brown vs. Board of Education* Supreme Court decision was a momentous court case with respect to the civil rights movement; it laid the foundation for ending legalized segregation in the Southern United States. The NAACP, in 1951, asked on behalf of the Brown family, to end segregation in the Topeka Public School system. Though the case did not result in an immediate victory, it laid the footing for school desegregation in some Southern states. It did ultimately win the 1954 Supreme Court ruling, outlawing segregation (Friedman and McGarvie, 2003).

1960s AND 1970s

In the 1960s some of the most important social legislation took place. A list of some of the key new federal entitlements and policies passed included

- The Social Security Amendments of 1965, created Medicare and Medicaid and expanded Social Security benefits for widows, retirees, college-aged students, and the disabled. Medicaid is a jointly funded, Federal-State health insurance program created for needy and low-income individuals. It provides coverage for children, the elderly, individuals who are blind, disabled, and others who are eligible to collect federally assisted income maintenance payments.
- The Food Stamp Act of 1964 provided food assistance to those with limited incomes to get a greater share food abundance of the United States.
- The Economic Opportunity Act of 1964 created the Job Corps, the Head Start program, the Volunteers in Service to America (VISTA) program, and the federal work-study program just to name a few.
- The Elementary and Secondary Education Act (ESEA) of 1965 created the Title I program subsidizing school districts that had a substantial share of disadvantaged students. ESEA has been reauthorized into the No Child Left Behind Act. Furthermore, America launched its "War on Poverty".
- The Title XX amendment to the Social Security Act in 1975 provided for the purchase of social services, training, and housing for persons who qualified based on their income.

The civil rights movement, and specifically NAACP and the Urban League, were instrumental in forcing action. The NAACP's capability to assist in the political process needed to influence social reform and change is the basis of the civil rights movement's ability to influence large-scale policy change today.

The Child Abuse Prevention and Treatment Act, passed in 1974, and the Education for All Handicapped Children Act in 1975, mandated that all public schools provided disabled children with education comparable to that of other children. The Child Abuse and Prevention Act of 1974 increased the number of children who were identified as suffering from child maltreatment and entered the foster care system. It became apparent that guidelines were needed for safe permanent living arrangements for children in out-of-home care, due to this increase in these clients. Prior to 1980 many children were placed in foster care homes without a sense of permanency or sufficient planning; the Adoptions Assistance and Child Welfare Act of 1980 (AACWA) delivered programs to better address children's needs.

1980s AND 1990s

During the presidency of Ronald Reagan (1981–1989), the administration emphasized economic values that were of a conservative nature, beginning with Reagan's implementation of supply-side economic policies, labeled Reaganomics. Reagan's policies involved the largest tax cut in American history and increased defense spending as part of his tactic against the Soviet Union. The Omnibus Budget Reconciliation Act (OBRA) of 1981 gave more authority and less funding to states for public assistance programs and let states determine eligibility for these programs. The Tax Equity and Fiscal Responsibility Act of 1982 resulted in decreased Medicare, Medicaid, AFDC, Supplemental Security Income (SSI), and unemployment funds.

When President Clinton took office (1993–2001) the first law he signed was the Family and Medical Leave Act; this act guaranteed that parents could take up to 12 weeks of unpaid leave to take care of a sick relative or newborn baby without risking losing their jobs. In addition, the Earned Income Tax Credit was expanded to provide a larger benefit to families that worked and allowed childless workers to also benefit. Congress, in 1996, passed a 20% increase in the minimum wage, which improved wages for almost 10 million Americans. Under Clinton, nutritional support and better housing was provided for low-income families. In 1997, a child tax credit was established; this directly reduced a family's income tax bill by $500 per child.

Federal funding for public school education increased from $8.5 billion to over $11 billion dollars. This increase was reinforced by the Improving America's Schools Act, which reauthorized the Elementary and Secondary Education Act to increase responsibility in schools by assisting low-income students and permitting the incorporation of technology into curricula. In 1997, the Hope Scholarship tax credit and the Lifetime Learning tax credit were passed to help cover the costs of college tuition.

THE 21st CENTURY AND BEYOND

On September 11, 2001, terrorist attacks occurred. President Bush answered these attacks by launching an international military campaign, which included the war in Afghanistan in 2001 and the war in Iraq in 2003, referred to as the "War on Terror." Bush signed the Patriot Act and No Child Left Behind Act into law, and cut Medicare prescription drug benefits for seniors and funding for the President's Emergency Plan for AIDS Relief (PEPFAR). George W. Bush increased privatization and decreased government funding for social programs to offset deficits that occurred as a result of tax cuts, the Iraq war, and natural disasters (e.g., Hurricane Katrina).

Barack Obama, the first African American president, signed the Affordable Care Act, referred to as "Obamacare," which aimed to provide universal access to health insurance for all Americans. In addition, in response to the Great Recession, a period of general economic decline observed in world markets during the late 2000s and early 2010s Obama signed into law economic stimulus legislation in the form of the American Recovery and Reinvestment

Act of 2009, the Tax Relief Job Creation Act of 2010, and the Unemployment Insurance Reauthorization. The expanded aid for low-income Americans during his presidency echoes Obama's aim of leveraging government power to fight income inequality.

CHAPTER EXERCISES

1. Do you believe the Elizabethan Poor Laws still influence some of the government assistance that is provided today in the United States? If so, please name which social welfare programs.

2. How do you believe the presidents discussed in this chapter impacted social service delivery during their presidency?

3. Identify differences in liberal versus conservative perspectives in regards to the delivery and support of social services.

4. Identify the current political scene and social justice issues in the United States today.

REFERENCES

Axinn, J. & Stern, M. J. (2005). *Social welfare: A history of the American response to need. 6th Ed.* Boston: Allyn & Bacon.

Friedman, L. J. & McGarvie, M. D. (Eds.). (2003). *Charity, philanthropy, and civility in American history.* New York, NY: Cambridge University Press.

Harris, J. L. (1992). *History and achievement of the NAACP.* New York, NY: Scholastic Library Publishing.

National Association of Social Workers. (2016). *NASW Social Work Pioneers* http://www.naswfoundation.org/pioneers/r/richmond.html

National Association of Social Workers (NASW) (1973). Addams, Jane. *Twenty Years at Hull-House.* Washington, DC: Author.

IMAGE CREDIT

PART 2

SOCIAL WORK PRACTICE

3

SOCIAL WORK GENERALIST PRACTICE

LEARNING OBJECTIVES

This chapter focuses on assisting students with learning the key components of generalist practice. After reading this chapter, the reader will be able to

- identify central features of generalist practice,
- identify key social work theories that guide social work practice, and
- classify and identify the different roles in which social workers function.

KNOWLEDGE BASE

It is essential for students to have a knowledge base that links social work practice and applied knowledge in regard to human behavior in the social environment; economic, political, and social environments; and c) research.

Listed below are several courses that help build that knowledge base, with a short description of each.

Human Behavior in the Social Environment studies human development over the life span from a multidimensional perspective. Psychological, biological, sociological, and spiritual theories serve as frameworks to better comprehend the interrelationship of behavior and environmental contexts. Learning about human behavior in its environmental context is central to effective social work practice. Though all behavior is not consistently predictable, there are some commonly shared and anticipated aspects that enrich one's understanding of this interrelationship between human behavior and environmental impact.

Social Work Research offers an in depth understanding of a scientific, analytic method to increase knowledge for social work practice and for evaluating multi-level service delivery. The purpose of this course is the attainment of beginning-level knowledge, skills, and values necessary for conducting research in all direct practice settings.

History of Social Welfare Policy enhances students' awareness of the historical and contemporary social forces that affect policy development. Students learn how to assess and analyze social welfare policies from social work perspectives. Students also gain knowledge about the interrelationship of social welfare policies and the processes of oppression and discrimination.

Race, Ethnicity, and Diversity examines the socially constructed concept of *diversity* and how it shapes and impacts the formation of one's identity. Diversity encompasses the intersection of multiple factors such as class, race, age, color, culture, ethnicity, disability, sex, sexual orientation, gender, gender identity and expression, political ideology, immigration status, and religion. The course examines how all of these factors interact within the context of understanding the multicultural nature of global and American society.

Field Education and Field Work integrates classroom knowledge with applied field experiences. Field education provides an opportunity for students to discuss their field experiences with field staff and faculty and integrate them with knowledge gained from other core social work courses. Focus is given to providing opportunities to analyze pragmatic and procedural aspects of developing a professional self and acquiring skills necessary for generalist practice.

WHAT IS GENERALIST PRACTICE?

Practitioners who are generalists use a professional problem solving process to educate, engage, assess, advocate, counsel, and broker services with and on behalf of clients. These social workers work with individuals, families, groups, communities, and organizations in a variety of settings. They work with clients from a strengths perspective in an effort to support, recognize and build on the uniqueness of all individuals. The NASW Code of Ethics guides generalist social work practice and is committed to improving the well-being of all.

Some central features of generalist practice include

- planned change process,
- strengths based approach,
- client empowerment,
- person in environment, and
- multiple levels of intervention.

The *planned change process* is a problem solving technique that entails four steps: engagement, assessment, intervention, and evaluation.

- **Engagement Phase**: Here the social worker spends time getting to know the client, establishing trust, rapport, and laying the groundwork for collaboration.
- **Assessment**: In this phase the social worker collects, organizes, and interprets client data. Both the social worker and client identify the problem and jointly create agreed-upon intervention goals and objectives. Social workers assess client strengths and limitations and select the appropriate intervention.
- **Intervention**: Social worker initiates steps and actions to achieve goals and implement interventions that enhance client capacities. Goals are established and steps are identified to meet those goals. This phase involves helping clients resolve problems; social workers may mediate, negotiate, and advocate for their clients.
- **Evaluation:** The social worker critically analyzes, monitors, and evaluates interventions that were set with the client. This information is necessary in order to determine if the interventions are making a difference.

MULTIPLE LEVELS OF INTERVENTION

Social work is separated into three broad practice categories: micro, mezzo, and macro.

- Micro social work is the most common practice, and involves working with an individual or family (micro = individual).
- Mezzo social work occurs on an intermediate scale, involving working with small groups, neighborhoods, and institutions (mezzo = families and groups).
- Macro level social work involves interventions provided on a large scale that impact whole communities (macro = organizations and communities).

Fig 3.1

The Ecomap Diagram Form

Surname: _____

Date Completed: _____

Completed By: _____

Family Location: State, City, Neighborhood _____

Instruction: Draw lines connecting central Members of House to Members of Secondary Network using this key:

Strong: = = =   Stressful: ΔΔΔΔΔ

Tenuous: - - - - -   Flow of Resources: ~ ~ ~ ~ ~

| | Employment | Sociocultural |

Physical Wellness and Care	Secondary Network	
Social Welfare	Members of Household	Educational Institution

| Extracurricular Activity | | Close Acquaintances |

THEORIES USED IN THE SOCIAL WORK PROFESSION

There are many social work theories that guide social work practice. The following major theories are some that are commonly used in the field of social work.

Systems theory offers insights into human behavior in terms of complex systems, and offers a holistic understanding of individuals within an environment. Systems theory is used in situations where several systems are greatly connected and influence one another. It emphasizes the reciprocal relationships and the interrelationships of elements in nature (Teater, 2010).

Social learning theory is grounded on Albert Bandura's view that learning occurs through observation and imitation. This theory focuses on mediating processes that occur between stimuli and responses. Behavior is learned from the environment through the process of observational learning. New behavior will stay if it is reinforced (Bandura, 1977).

Psychosocial development theory was developed by Erik Erikson and is an eight-stage theory of identity and psychosocial development. According to this theory, individuals go through eight stages of development over the lifetime: hope, will, purpose, competence, fidelity, love, care, and wisdom. Each stage is divided into age ranges starting with infancy and ending in older adulthood (McLeod, 2013).

Psychodynamic theory was developed by Sigmund Freud and describes personality in terms of unconscious and conscious forces. It focuses on internal processes such as drives, needs, and emotions and how they motivate human behavior. It defines the personality as comprised of the id (basic instincts), the superego (follows rules and morals), and the ego (mediates between the id and the ego). Conscious and unconscious mental activity are forces that motivate an individual's behavior. Early childhood experiences play a significant role in the patterning of an individual's emotions, and are central to problems of living throughout life (Sharf, 2012).

Transpersonal theory: according to this theory, in individuals with healthy egos, stages in adulthood contribute to creativity, wisdom, and altruism. Psychosis can occur in people lacking healthy ego development. In addition, this theory offers an insight into how the spiritual and religious aspects of human existence can be understood, and how development builds upon and goes beyond biopsychosocial development (Davis, 2000).

Conflict theory brings attention to conflict, oppression, and dominance in the client's life and identifies how some individuals and groups try to advance their own interests over the interests of others. According to this theory, the social order is maintained by the dominant group's manipulation and control of non-dominant groups (Goroff, 1978).

Feminist theory emphasizes and recognizes how oppression and sexism play a part in a female's presenting problem due to the inequity in political, social, and economic structures that shape societies. This theory identifies the importance of gender and how it is essential when identifying the impact of domination and oppression in our society (Kemp & Brandwein, 2010; Abramovitz, 1994).

Cognitive behavioral therapy (CBT) is a time-limited structured approach to psychotherapy; it addresses the client's current problems (Dobson & Dobson, 2009). CBT utilizes problem-focused behavioral and cognitive strategies based on empirical science and builds on theories of cognition and learning (Craske, 2010). Interventions are provided within a collaborative method where professionals and clients work together to identify problems, set goals, develop intervention strategies, and evaluate the strategies. In the CBT model the client is viewed as having abilities and strengths to be an active agent with respect to change.

THEORETICAL PERSPECTIVES

There are many social work perspectives that inform social work practice. The following are some of the major perspectives that are generally used in the field of social work.

Strengths perspective: This theory originates from the work of Saleebey (2009). Here, the social worker believes that the client has multiple strengths that can assist him or her in working on their presenting problem(s). In addition, it focuses on the client's right to self-determination and identification of one's strengths. It is a philosophy that views the client as resourceful and resilient in the face of adversity. Unfortunately, the social worker may be the first person in the client's life who helps them identify their areas of strength. Often society focuses on the problems and on what is going wrong rather than the strengths that one has to overcome this problem or obstacle. Deficit based or problem focused models tend to keep the attention of the practitioner and the client on the problem instead of on the solution.

Ecological perspective has is origins in biological theories that examine how organisms adapt to their environments. The social work profession has expanded this perspective by examining how individuals, families, cultures, communities, and policies identify and intervene on strengths and weaknesses in the transactional processes between these systems (Germain, 1973).

Afrocentric perspective is a framework that values an African-centered worldview as the basis for theories and models of practice. It emphasizes customs of African cultures and how they pervaded the history, culture, and behavior of American culture. This perspective assists the social worker in considering the impact of historical events, policies, and behaviors of the African American experiences and social events in the lives of people of African descent (Asante, 1998; Mazama, 2003; Reid-Merritt, 2009).

MODELS IN SOCIAL WORK

Problem solving: This model aims to provide an understanding of the problem, brainstorm possible solutions, have the client pick a solution, implement the solution, and then evaluate how the solution worked.

Task-centered: This model breaks down the client's problem into small tasks so the client is more apt to work on it. Rehearsal, deadlines, and contracts are used to aid the client in feeling successful and motivated towards working to solve the problem.

Solution-focused: This model begins with the solution and then assists the client in establishing the steps that will lead to the solution. The model uses the miracle question to help clients envision what they want to obtain in their future. The miracle question focuses on imagining what the client's preferred future would be like and trying to work towards that future in a step-by-step way.

Narrative: This model uses letters and other methods to help the client re-write their lives.

KEY SOCIAL WORK CONCEPTS

Client empowerment is when social workers help to empower clients by providing them with knowledge and skills. The strengths based approach is one piece of client empowerment, in that it helps boost self-awareness and self-esteem. Empowerment is both a process and an outcome. Through the process of enhancing the power of individuals, groups, and communities, these entities are motivated to action. Their increased sense of power and of accomplishment is the outcome.

Self-determination is a feature of client empowerment that places emphases on informing clients of all options in order to make the most informed decisions for themselves. The belief is held that the client is capable of making choices and decisions. The social worker supports, educates, and encourages the client in this process.

Person-in-environment is rooted in the belief that an individual has reciprocal relationships with different aspects of that individual's environment (social, political, familial, temporal, spiritual, economic, and physical). It is a framework for assessing a client and his or her presenting problem, and strengths the client possesses.

Evidence Based Practice involves using approaches that have been empirically tested using rigorous research methodology.

SOCIAL WORK ROLES

Social workers function in many roles as they offer support and services. These roles are not exclusive, and a typical day of services to one client may incorporate multiple roles. Some of the roles of social workers include initiator, activist, group facilitator, advocate, educator, case manager, enabler, broker, counselor, mediator, and evaluator.

- Initiator: recognizes a problem and calls attention to it
- Activist: takes action for change on behalf of others to promote social justice
- Group facilitator: takes a leadership role within task and treatment groups
- Advocate: promotes the client's position or need
- Mobilizer: organizes and empowers community members to achieve goals
- Educator: provides information and teaches skills
- Case manager: coordinates the services and resources of multiple agencies
- Enabler: helps build the capacity of clients to deal with challenges
- Broker: links clients with needed resources
- Counselor: helps clients identify problems and intervention strategies
- Mediator: serves in a dispute resolution mode between two parties
- Evaluator: collects data to determine the effectiveness of interventions

Consider the following example case:

The Salem family has recently sought assistance at the agency where you work due to moving to the United States from their native country, Egypt. Mrs. Salem has been able to find employment as a waitress, but does not earn enough to both pay the rent and purchase enough food for the family of four. Dr. Salem was a medical physician in Egypt, but his medical degree and medical license is not valid here in the United States. Dr. Salem is exhibiting signs of depression, and his temper has become very short with his wife and two children. The couple has come to the local mental health center for support.

- The social worker may serve as a broker by linking the family with the resources to apply for food stamps, provide information on local food pantries, or both.
- As an initiator, the social worker may be aware of several families in a similar situation, and start a support group for men who are looking for work.
- Then, the social worker would serve as group facilitator for that group. As a counselor the social worker may provide individual therapy for Dr. Salem to help him identify strategies to cope with his depression, and serve as an educator by teaching him stress management skills.
- By asking Dr. Salem for a self-rating of his level of depression each week, the social worker serves as evaluator to determine the effectiveness of interventions.

TOOLS OF THE TRADE: ECOMAPS AND GENOGRAMS

ECOMAP

The ecomap was developed by Ann Hartman in 1975 as a tool to help social workers understand the interrelatedness of their clients' different relationships and the impact these social systems have on the clients' themselves, and on their presenting issues. Ecomaps are visual representations that provide a view of the relationships and influences between individuals, families or collectives, and their ecological environment, including their social networks. Ecomaps are commonly used in individual and family therapy as a tool for organizing information to assist with assessment, planning and intervention. They depict the nature of relationships and highlight the flow or these relationships or lack of resources. Ecomaps are developed with the client or clients in an effort to gain multiple perspectives, to support engagement, and to build rapport. This process assists in building awareness, strengthens relationships and their influence, and provides insights leading to self-reflection.

Fig 3.2

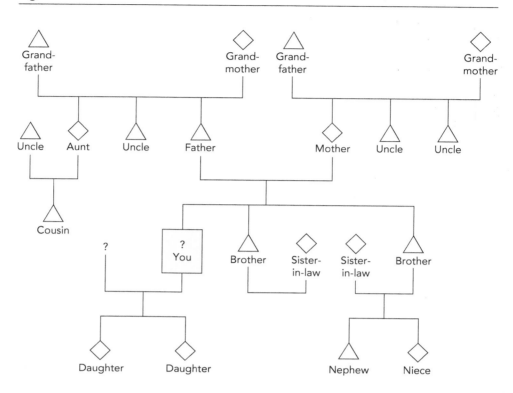

GENOGRAM

A genogram is a graphic representation of a family tree, created with symbols that define and describe connections and relationships between an extended family. Social workers construct genograms with clients to provide a better understanding of relationships and identify patterns between them. Figure 3.2 is a genogram of three generations of a client who is married and has two siblings and two children. The yellow box represents the client. Genograms usually consist of three generations of the client's family, like the one above; they have symbols to represent gender, types of relationships, pregnancy, etc.

CHAPTER EXERCISES

1. Identify and define the three levels of intervention in social work.

2. Name three social work theories that guide social work practice.

3. Explain when and why a social worker would use the Afrocentric perspective.

4.   Draw an ecomap for the Salem family described on page 35.

5.   Name and define the four steps of the planned change process.

REFERENCES

Abramovitz, Mimi. (1996). *Regulating the lives of women: Social welfare policy from the colonial times to the present.* Boston, MA: South End Press.

Asante, M. (1998). *The Afrocentric idea: Revised and expanded edition.* Philadelphia, PA: Temple University Press.

Bandura, A. (1977). *Social learning theory.* Englewood Cliffs, NJ: Prentice Hall.

Craske, M. G. (2010). *Cognitive-behavioral therapy.* Washington, D.C.: American Psychological Association.

Davis, J. (2000). "We Keep Asking Ourselves, What is Transpersonal Psychology?" *Guidance and Counselling, 15* (3).

Germain, B.C. (1973). "An Ecological Perspective in Case-work Practice," *Casework,* 54: 323–330.

Goroff, N. N. (1978). "Conflict Theories and Social Work Education". *Journal of Sociology & Social Welfare, 5* (6).

Kemp, S. P., & Brandwein, R. (2010). Feminism and social work in the United States: An intertwined history. *Journal of Women and Social Work, 25* (4), 341–364. DOI:10.1177/0886109910384075

Mazama, A. (2003). *The Afrocentric paradigm.* Trenton, New Jersey: Africa World Press, Inc.

McLeod, S. A. (2013). Erik Erikson. Retrieved from www.simplypsychology.org/Erik-Erikson.html

National Association of Social Workers. (2005). *Social workers in private practice: A reference guide.* Washington, DC: Author.

Reid-Merritt, P. (2010). *Righteous self-determination: The Black social work movement in America.* Baltimore, MD: Black Classic Press.

Saleebey, D. (2009). *Strengths perspective in social work practice, 5th edition.* Pearson, University of Kansas.

4

VALUES AND CODE OF ETHICS IN SOCIAL WORK PRACTICE

LEARNING OBJECTIVES

Chapter 4 focuses on assisting students with learning key components of the social work profession's values and code of ethics. After reading this chapter, the reader will be able to

- identify the social work profession's code of ethics that guide social work practice, and
- be familiar with ethical and professional behaviors that include key values, ethics and concepts that ground social work practice.

SOCIAL WORK VALUES AND CODE OF ETHICS

Social workers seek to enhance the capacity of people to address their own needs. The profession is a distinct field of practice from all of the helping professions because it looks at the individual as a whole within a strengths perspective. It draws upon ethics, values, principles, practice methods and person-in-environment perspective as essential components of the profession. Its set of core values include belief in the inherent dignity and worth of the person, service to the profession and to society, seeking social justice for all, and understanding the importance of human relationships.

The chief mission of the social work profession is to enhance human well-being and assist in meeting the basic human needs of all people, with specific attention to empowering individuals who are oppressed, vulnerable, and living in poverty. What is unique to the profession is the attention given to the environmental forces that create, and address problems in living. Over more than 100 years, social workers have helped millions of individuals challenge their circumstances and change their lives, and helped institutions value and support individuals in need.

According to the International Federation of Social Workers, the definition of social work is as follows:

> The social work profession promotes social change, problem solving in human relationships and the empowerment and liberation of people to enhance well-being. Utilizing theories of human behavior and social systems, social work intervenes at the points where people interact with their environments. Principles of human rights and social justice are fundamental to social work. (http://www.ifsw.org/en/p38000208.html)

The National Association of Social Workers, NASW, established in 1955, is the largest membership organization of professional social workers, having over 132,000 members. The NASW aims at enhancing the professional growth and development of its members, to produce and uphold professional standards, and to advance social policies. The NASW adopted its first Code of Ethics in 1960 and there have only been two major revisions of the code since then. The first took place in 1979, and the second major revision was approved by the 1996 NASW Delegate Assembly. This version of the *NASW Code of Ethics* is still in place today, with some revisions by the 2008 NASW Delegate Assembly that added language related to issues of sexual orientation and gender identity as they relate to cultural competency, respect, discrimination, and social/ political action. The mission of the social work profession is articulated in the Preamble to the Code of Ethics of the National Association of Social Workers:

> The primary mission of the social work profession is to enhance human well-being and help meet the basic human needs of all people, with particular attention to the needs and empowerment of people who are vulnerable, oppressed, and living in poverty. A historic and defining feature of social work is the profession's focus on individual well-being in a social context and the well-being of society.

The *NASW Code of Ethics* includes four sections:

- Preamble,
- Purpose of the *NASW Code of Ethics*,

- Ethical Principles, and
- Ethical Standards.

PREAMBLE

The preamble states "The primary mission of the social work profession is to enhance human well-being and help meet the basic human needs of all people, with particular attention to the needs and empowerment of people who are vulnerable, oppressed, and living in poverty." The preamble also classifies the core values of the profession, which serve as the foundation of the profession's unique perspective and purpose.

The full *NASW Code of Ethics* can be found on the NASW Web site at http://www.social-workers.org/.

PURPOSE OF THE *NASW CODE OF ETHICS*

This section identifies six overall purposes of the *NASW Code of Ethics*.

- Identify core values on which social work's mission is based.
- Summarize broad ethical principles that reflect the profession's core values and establish a set of specific ethical standards that should be used to guide social work practice.
- Help social workers identify relevant considerations when professional obligations conflict or ethical uncertainties arise.
- Provide ethical standards to which the general public can hold the social work profession accountable.
- Socialize practitioners new to the field to social work's mission, values, ethical principles, and ethical standards.
- Articulate standards that the social work profession itself can use to assess whether social workers have engaged in unethical conduct.

ETHICAL PRINCIPLES

The ethical principles "set forth ideals to which all social workers should aspire."

- Social workers' primary goal is to help people in need and to address social problems.
- Social workers challenge social justice.
- Social workers respect the inherent dignity and worth of the person.
- Social workers recognize the central importance of human relationships.

- Social workers behave in a trustworthy manner.
- Social workers practice within their areas of competence and develop and enhance their professional expertise.

ETHICAL STANDARDS

The Ethical Standards section outlines social workers' ethical responsibilities in six categories:

- to clients,
- to colleagues,
- in practice settings,
- as professionals,
- to the social work profession, and
- to the broader society.

PROFESSIONAL VALUES

Adhering to professional values is a central feature of social work practice. Social workers must be aware with his or her own values, and control for inappropriate imposition into practice situations. Though our own values are usually set and can be a very important part of ourselves, the social work profession does not ask nor require us to change or deny those values, but rather encourages the professional to be cognizant of them so that they do not affect or hinder the therapeutic relationship with a client.

Professionalism is integral to values and ethics of social work and includes seven areas:

- sophisticated knowledge, competence, self-efficacy, and expertise;
- respect for and adhering to the values of the social work profession and its code of ethics;
- personal and professional integrity, self-understanding and self-control, and social support;
- critical thinking, scientific inquiry, and career-long learning;
- engagement in diversity and respect for difference;
- advancement of human rights and social justice; and
- promotion of social well-being.

The profession's mission is embedded in a set of core values. These core values are the foundation of social work's unique perspective and purpose.

THE PROFESSIONAL USE OF SELF IN SOCIAL WORK

The development of one's professional identity and the professional use of self are interconnected. The use of self in social work practice is the relating of values, knowledge, and skills attained in social work education with facets of one's personal self, including cultural heritage, belief systems, personality traits, and life experiences (Dewane, 2006).

An aspect of how one's *self-influences* one's social work practice is the individual's belief system. A belief system is the way an individual understands, organizes, and makes sense of the world, i.e., one's worldview. It is essential for social work students to assess their worldview; even seasoned social workers must always take inventory regarding their changing worldview. Human beings are not stagnant and neither are our views. Many times, experiences, age, and world events just to name a few, impact and can alter one's perspectives on presenting issues that will impact our clients. By defining our worldview, we are more apt to recognize the similarity between our personal values with those of the social work profession and of our clients.

Another advantage to defining one's worldview is that it enables the social workers to recognize if they are imposing their own values onto the client and failing to adhere to the core value of self-determination. This professional error occurs because the social worker has not thoroughly examined his or her own values and beliefs, and unconsciously imposes their worldview on the client. It is essential that social workers recognize if they are holding too rigidly to their own values and failing to honoring two of the profession's key values: self-determination and respect.

ETHICAL DILEMMAS

An ethical dilemma occurs when two conflicting values or obligations are present in the same situation. For example, there could be a conflict between the client's right to self-determination and the safety of the client, between personal and professional values, or between confidentiality and duty to inform. Ethical dilemmas can take place across the range of practice settings and at all levels of social work practice.

The ethical decision making process in social work involves taking into consideration all the values, principles, and standards that the profession abides by that are relevant to a scenario in which ethical judgment is warranted. Social workers' choices and actions must be consistent with the code of ethics. The *NASW Code of Ethics* serves as a frame of reference by NASW members, individuals, agencies, organizations, and other bodies (such as professional liability insurance providers, courts of law, licensing and regulatory boards, agency boards of directors, government agencies, and other professional groups). Social workers must be mindful of the implications of violation of the code of ethics; violation of standards does not automatically result in a legal charge or violation of the law. Alleged violations of the Code are subjected to a peer review process.

Social workers should be aware of any conflicts between personal and professional values and deal with them responsibly. Situations can occur when social workers' ethical obligations conflict with agency policies or relevant laws. When this occurs, it is essential for the social worker to make some accountable efforts to find resolution that is consistent with the standards set in this Code. The *NASW Code of Ethics* represents the commitment of all social workers to uphold the Code and to act ethically.

ETHICAL PRINCIPLES

The following ethical principles are based on the profession's set of core values that professionals should aim to abide by:

Fig 4.1

Core Values of the Social Work Profession

CORE VALUES OF SOCIAL WORK IDENTIFIED IN THE PREAMBLE OF THE *NASW CODE OF ETHICS* ARE:

Service: The profession's principal goal is to aid people in need and to address social problems. Social workers use knowledge, values, and skills to assist individuals in need and to address social problems.

Social Justice: Social workers seek social change regarding vulnerable and oppressed individuals and groups of people and challenge any social injustices that exist in society. Social workers' social change efforts typically focus on issues of poverty, discrimination, unemployment, and other forms of social injustice.

Dignity and Worth of the Person: A core value, respecting the inherent dignity and worth of the person is an essential component of the profession. The profession aims at treating each individual in a respectful manner while being mindful of differences and cultural and ethnic diversity. In addition, another core value that relates is to this value is supporting client self-determination, the right of individuals to make their own choices.

Importance of Human Relationships: Recognizing the essential significance of human relationships is another key component. Social workers view the impact of relationships and how they can serve as important vehicles for change. Social seek to strengthen relationships among individuals in an effort to restore, promote, maintain, and enhance well-being of individuals, families, social groups, organizations, and communities.

Integrity: Social workers are mindful of the profession's mission, ethical principles, values, and ethical standards and practice in a manner consistent with them, hence behaving in a trustworthy manner.

Competence: It is expected that social workers practice within their areas of competence and develop their professional expertise. Social workers continually strive to increase their professional knowledge and skills and to apply them in practice. In addition, social workers should aspire to add to the knowledge base of the profession.

The following case is an example of a common ethical dilemma that a social worker will face when working with a client who is a victim of domestic violence:

Michelle Wilson, a 30-year-old female who has been married for 10 years has just disclosed to her social worker that her husband routinely physically and sexually abuses her. Michelle states she is worried about her safety but is not ready to leave her husband because she loves him.

In this situation, the ethical dilemma for the social worker can be the following:

- Dignity and Worth of the Person—though one may find the need to support the right to self-determination.
- Importance of Human Relationship—Breaching a client's confidentiality can affect their trust moving forward (protecting others, welfare always takes precedence in this situation).
- Integrity—Social workers must behave in a trustworthy manner, with our clients and with the communities we serve. (We must protect those in society when we know harm is being done or will be done to them.)

Many times when faced with an ethical dilemma, there is no easy right answer. The professional must decide what's best for their client and their practice.

BREACHES OF CONFIDENTIALITY WITH CLIENTS

There comes a time when every social worker will hear the question, "You're not going to report me, are you?" The social worker abides by the code of ethics with respect to keeping confidentiality, but must break this code in the three following situations:

- Client wants to hurt themselves.
- Client wants to hurt someone else.
- Client is abusing (physical, sexual, neglect) their child.

Another common ethical dilemma encountered by social workers is the right to confidentiality versus the right to self-determination, particularly in cases of suicidal clients. In this scenario, the social worker must respect their clients' right to privacy and confidentiality, and may not divulge any information about clients without his/her prior, written consent. Social workers must also respect a client's right to self-determination. Though, in cases of suicide or the threat of harm to another person, or cases of child abuse, a social worker is obligated to break confidentiality to protect her client and the public.

STEPS FOR HANDLING ETHICAL DILEMMAS

1. Consult the *Code of Ethics*

Social workers should always have a copy of the *NASW Code of Ethics* handy. Every professional in the field should have thorough knowledge of the *Code of Ethics* in order to be able to identify any principles that come into conflict with their cases.

2. Review State and Federal Laws

Social workers must be sure that their decisions are sound, not only ethically but also legally. Be mindful, that if a social worker acts in an unethical manner, they are putting themselves in a position to lose their license or even their freedom.

3. Seek Supervision

Seeking supervision is essential regardless of how long one has been in the field; particularly when there are any doubts, questions, or if you just need a sounding board, seek supervision. Everyone needs a second opinion once in a while. Supervisors can be particularly helpful in providing professional guidance.

4. Consult the NASW

Most states have a hotline social workers can call when they experience ethical dilemmas. A hotline offers confidentiality to the professional and provides professional advice on how to handle things.

5. Take Time to Process What You've Learned

After proper research and consultation has been sufficiently done, take some time to process the situation before making any decisions. Taking time allows the social worker to be at ease with the decision that was made to handle this ethical dilemma.

CHAPTER EXERCISES

1. Identify why ethical dilemmas occur in the social work profession.

2. Name two key features of the *Code of Ethics*.

3. Where do your values come from? Can you identify any personal values that conflict with the following social work values?

- Service
- Social justice
- Dignity and worth of the Individual
- Integrity
- Competence

REFERENCES

Dewane, C. J. (2006). Use of self: A primer revisited. *Clinical Social Work Journal, 34*(4), 543–558. DOI: 10.1007/s10615-005-0021-5

National Association of Social Workers. (1973). *NASW standards for social service manpower.* Washington, DC: Author.

IMAGE CREDIT

Fig. 4.1: Source: National Association of Social Workers; Adapted by Allison Sinanan.

PART 3

CULTURAL COMPETENCE: WORKING WITH OPPRESSED POPULATIONS

5

WHAT IS CULTURAL COMPETENCE AND WHY IS IT IMPORTANT?

LEARNING OBJECTIVES

Chapter 5 focuses on assisting students in understanding cultural competence and why it is a key component of the social work profession. After reading this chapter, the reader will be able to

- identify how cultural competence guides the social work profession, and
- be familiar with how to work effectively with diverse populations.

WHAT IS CULTURAL COMPETENCE AND WHY IS IT IMPORTANT?

The United States is constantly undergoing significant demographic changes. From 1990 to 2010 the population growth had an increase in people of color. Cultural diversity in the United States impacts all aspects of social work practice, including the goal of delivering culturally competent services to a broad range of clientele.

Cultural diversity has primarily been associated with race and ethnicity, though diversity in social work also includes the sociocultural experiences of people of different ages, classes, sexual orientation, religious and spiritual beliefs, and physical and mental abilities. Therefore, cultural competence in social work practice requires increased consciousness of how clients experience their uniqueness and handle their similarities and differences within a larger social context.

CULTURAL COMPETENCE: WHAT IS IT?

Cultural competence in social work is well-defined as the practice by which social work professionals act in a respectful professional manner to all clients regardless of their ethnic backgrounds, cultures, classes, languages, religions, and other diversity factors that protect the dignity of each person. The social work profession gives great importance to culturally sensitive practice. Cultural competence enables social workers to have effective interactions with clients whose cultures differ from their own. It enables clients to feel good about their interactions with their social worker, and it allows all to accomplish their goals in the therapeutic process. Race and ethnicity have an impact on professional relations, and inadequate cultural competence results in less effective services. A client who has a social worker of a different ethnicity may assume that the worker will not truly understand or relate to the client's worldview; this may decrease the likelihood that the client will continue services. The reverse is also true. Social workers often have a poorer opinion of those clients whom they see as having significantly different views from themselves. This dynamic is less common in less prejudiced individuals (Davis & Proctor, 1989).

Cultural competence involves being aware and respectful of the values, beliefs, traditions, customs, and parenting styles of those we serve, while understanding that there is often a wide a range of differences within groups and between them. It involves being aware of how our own culture influences how we view others. Cultural competence in social work is not something that the professional attains simply by attending a class or workshop, but rather it is developed over time through training, experience, guidance, and self-evaluation. The social worker must be committed to desire continuous learning in this realm. Cultural competence can best be described as a set of consistent attitudes, behaviors, and policies that enables professionals to effectively function across differences in cultures (Cross, 1988).

When attempting to learn about other cultures in an effort to become culturally competent, there are several things the professional can do: (a) read about the history, geography, poetry and people, as well as fiction about a particular culture; (b) participate in cultural rituals by learning and/or celebrating their holidays, working on community projects, and attending places of worship; (c) learn the language; (d) attend a cultural festival to learn about the food, clothing, and music of a particular culture. Doing all or some of these activities can improve the social worker's ability to challenge any false beliefs, assumptions, and stereotypes and to recognize that their way of doing things and thinking is not the only way.

The NASW and the Council of Social Work Education mandate professionals in the field to have the skills and knowledge needed for culturally competent practice. Cultural competence is viewed by the NASW as a tool for meeting professional expectations, improving the quality and delivery of social work services, and increasing the likelihood of better client outcomes and satisfaction with services.

THE NATIONAL ASSOCIATION OF SOCIAL WORKERS (NASW) AND THE CALL FOR CULTURAL COMPETENCE IN THE FIELD

The NASW (2010) identifies culturally appropriate service as a priority standard within all specialties of practice. The Council on Social Work Education (CSWE) (2015) also requires all accredited social work institutions to have diversity content in their curricula. The CSWE indicates that one of the purposes of social work education is to prepare "social workers to practice without discrimination, with respect, and with knowledge and skills related to clients' age, class, color, culture, disability, ethnicity, family structure, gender, marital status, national origin, race, religion, sex, and sexual orientation," and charges that graduates must demonstrate the ability to practice in such a manner (CSWE, 2015). The social work profession has adopted a commitment to diversity, affirmative action and inclusion. However, statistics show social workers in the United States are predominantly White (88.5 percent) and female (78.0 percent). Social work client populations are more diverse than the professionals that serve them. In many cases, services provided to clients are largely targeted to marginalized communities and special populations, groups that include disproportionately high numbers of people of color, the elderly, individuals with disabilities, and clients of lower socioeconomic status; therefore an emphasis is placed on the need for professionals to be culturally competent. The NASW has a National Committee on Racial and Ethnic Diversity (NASW, 2010) that identifies 10 standards for cultural competence, which are listed below:

1. **Ethics and values:** Social workers respect the client and the right to self-determination, and deals with any ethical dilemmas that may arise adhering to the *Code of Ethics*.

2. **Self-awareness:** Social workers need to be mindful of their own cultural identity and examine their own biases, attitudes, and beliefs about difference, which include a client's race, ethnicity, sexuality, sexual orientation, religion, and other cultural factors.

3. **Cross-cultural knowledge:** Social workers strive to be well informed about cultures other than their own.

4. **Cross-cultural skills:** Social workers must be knowledgeable about new information, skills, and interventions and know how to work effectively with clients who are different than them.

5. **Service delivery:** Social workers must ensure culturally competent services are provided and interact with other professionals to sustain awareness of cultural diversity.

6. **Empowerment and advocacy:** Social workers, duties include advocating for and with clients towards development of individual power, consciousness awareness, and social change.

7. **Diverse workforce:** Social workers advocate for diversity of professionals.

8. **Professional education:** Social workers promote education and training that put emphasis on cultural competence.

9. **Language diversity:** Social workers are obligated to provide services in the language of their clients' preference through bilingual and/or multilingual employees, or through the use of interpreters.

10. **Cross-cultural leadership:** Social workers are obligated to share the knowledge of the profession's ethics and values with other professions.

BECOMING CULTURALLY COMPETENT

As social workers, practicing in culturally sensitive ways is of the highest importance. The *NASW Code of Ethics* refers to cultural competence in section 1.05 reprinted below. http://www.socialworkers.org/pubs/Code/code.asp

1.05 Cultural Competence and Social Diversity

a. Social workers should understand culture and its function in human behavior and society, recognizing the strengths that exist in all cultures.

b. Social workers should have a knowledge base of their clients' cultures and be able to demonstrate competence in the provision of services that are sensitive to clients' cultures and to differences among people and cultural groups.

c. Social workers should obtain education about and seek to understand the nature of social diversity and oppression with respect to race, ethnicity, national origin, color, sex, sexual orientation, gender identity or expression, age, marital status, political belief, religion, immigration status, and mental or physical disability.

Cultural competence involves a heightened consciousness of how individuals experience and understanding their uniqueness, apply that awareness within practice, and deal with their differences and similarities within a larger social context. In an effort to be culturally competent, the following elements must be learned:

Fig 5.1

Key Components for Being Culturally Competent

Diversity	• Understanding of diversity between and within cultures
Consciousness	• Consciousness of the dynamics inherent when cultures interact
Values	• Understanding of how personal and professional values may conflict with or accommodate the needs of diverse clients
History	• Understanding of history, traditions, values, family systems and artistic expressions of diverse cultural groups
Research	• Methodological approaches, skills and techniques reflecting understanding of the role of culture in course content
Language	• Information in language appropriate to participants
Awareness	• Awareness involves being consciousness of one's personal reactions to people and situations that are different
Attitude	• Expression of one's beliefs and values related to culture and cultural differences
Knowledge	• Information contributing to self-awareness and improving cross-cultural effectiveness
Skills	• Specific strategies and behaviors, including both verbal and nonverbal communication, which contribute to the creation of inclusive systems

HOW IMPORTANT IS RECOGNIZING ONE'S OWN RACE/ETHNICITY IN BEING CULTURALLY COMPETENT?

Without cultural awareness, social workers can unintentionally contribute to the oppression that clients face. Social workers need skills to assess clients' entire ecosystems. The unintended consequence of inattention to clients' cultures can be that the social worker echoes society's oppression by assuming that clients need to change, rather than advocating for social change.

Identifying and truthfully knowing who you are influences how you interact with others, particularly in a professional setting with others who may differ from you. If social workers are to successfully encourage racial and ethnic pride with clients and are to demonstrate an understanding of the importance of race, culture, and ethnicity, this starts with knowing themselves.

It is essential for social workers to understand how difference and diversity shape the individual and shape the formation of one's identity. The significance of acknowledging and attaining knowledge about their own race and ethnic identity enables social workers to understand and work with all types of individuals who are trying to better themselves. According to Campinha-Bacote (2002) professionals should possess a cultural desire to know more about their client's cultural, racial, and ethnic groups. Cultural desire requires individuals to be self-motivated in wanting to engage in the process of cultural competence, rather than having to be coerced into doing so.

When assessing clients, social workers need to explore ethnicity. Assessments should include the influence of culture and how the client's community can be helpful. The assessment should also incorporate an understanding of the person in an environment, which requires learning about the client's birthplace, immigration experience, level of acculturation and assimilation, and language preference. Social workers must possess a willingness to talk about perceived and real differences, particularly about topics like racism, sexuality, classism, oppression, and religion, in an attempt to improve their cultural competence.

KEY ELEMENTS FOR ATTAINING CULTURAL COMPETENCE

SELF-AWARENESS

Self-awareness is a key feature in truly becoming culturally competent. Self-awareness involves increasing self-understanding and engaging in self-exploration. Since social workers need to be able to manage their thoughts and feelings, as well as words, gestures, and behaviors, they have to cultivate self-discipline and self-control. Without these two essential qualities social workers can unintentionally harm those they aim to aid. Appreciation of one's own culture is essential in order to have the ability to truly understand and appreciate the culture of others. A great question to start with is: What values do I have, and what culture or cultures do they come from? Self-understanding is an ongoing process that enables social workers to grow personally and professionally.

CULTURAL KNOWLEDGE

The civil rights movement involved African Americans, women, the gay and lesbian population, and other minority groups. These groups protested and informed the country of their long histories of oppression. Currently, the continuous growing number of immigrants in the United States provides the need and continuance for culturally competent practice. However, culturally competent services are needed beyond race and ethnicity. Culturally competent social workers are also better able to address issues of gender and help persons with disabilities, older adults, gays, lesbians, bisexuals, and transgender people.

Cultural knowledge involves social workers being aware of the interconnectedness between the socio-economic and socio-cultural realities faced by many clients. This simply means that the professional realizes how a client's exposure to poverty, crime, substandard housing, neighborhood conditions, racism, and discrimination are linked to poor health and mental health outcomes (Mechanic, 2005; Williams & Jackson, 2005).

LINGUISTIC COMPETENCE

Linguistic competence involves a commitment on the part of the social worker and the organization providing services to communicate in ways that the clientele prefer. Strategies that demonstrate linguistic competence include employing bilingual or multilingual social workers, interpreters, and having materials printed in other languages.

CROSS-CULTURAL KNOWLEDGE

Social workers shall have and continue to develop specialized knowledge and understanding about the history, traditions, values, family systems, and artistic expressions of major client groups served. Social workers need an understanding of their client's history in an effort to better understand the client's presenting problem(s).

CROSS-CULTURAL SKILLS

Social workers shall use appropriate methodological approaches, skills, and techniques that reflect the social workers' understanding of the role of culture in the helping process. These skills take into account how people from differing cultural backgrounds communicate, in similar and different ways among themselves, and how they attempt to communicate across cultures.

THEORETICAL PERSPECTIVES

Social workers need to understand the worldviews of the clients they serve and be cognizant of those who have power and privilege. By identifying who in our society has power and privilege prevents the professional from dismissing the experiences of the socially devalued marginalized groups in our society and what they must endure daily. We must also acknowledge the institutional racism that is present in our educational system, judicial system, places of employment, and the media. Identifying the different facets of where racism lives allows social workers to see clients in their totality. Of the many social work perspectives that inform the practice, below we list some of the major perspectives that are generally used to understand cultural competence in the field.

Fig 5.2

Theoretical Frameworks Commonly Used in Social Work Practice

THEORETICAL FRAMEWORKS	MAJOR CONTRIBUTIONS
Cross-Cultural Approach	A model of cognitive humanism that emphasizes the ethical and humanistic dimensions when counseling clients from diverse backgrounds.
Strengths Based Perspective	It enables the clients to use resources and become diversity empowered. The focus is on the strengths of clients rather than problems. Belief that positive perception of self-worth in the clinician is created through: 1. Recognition 2. Connection 3. Analysis 4. Knowledge and skills 5. Reflection and collaboration
Ethnic-Sensitive Practice	One's individual and collective history has an impact on understanding psychosocial problems. Social workers try to simultaneously focus their attention on the individual and systemic concerns as they emerge.
Person-in-Environment	Problems faced by clients are assessed in relation to their historical, environmental, cultural, family, and individual levels. Interactions of individuals with their environments occur at all of these levels, and any disruption results in stress. The emphasis is on educating social work students toward differences in the different ethnic/social groups.
Ecological Theory	The ecological theory looks at the individual, family, community, national, and global issues when examining the client's problems.

CHAPTER EXERCISES

1. Identify and define three elements the social worker must learn to become culturally competent.

2. List two standards the NASW charges social workers with attaining to become culturally competent.

3. Name a theory that helps social workers provide culturally appropriate interventions.

REFERENCES

Campinha-Bacote, J. (2002). The process of cultural competence in the delivery of healthcare services: A model of care. *Journal of Transcultural Nursing, 13,* 181–184.

Council on Social Work Education. (2015). *2015 Educational policy and accreditation standards (EPAS).* Retrieved from http://www.cswe.org/File.aspx?id=81660

Cross, T. I. (1989). *Toward a culturally competent system of care.* Washington, DC: CASSP Technical Assistance Center.

Mechanic, D. (2005). Policy challenges in addressing racial disparities and improving population health. *Health Affairs, 24*(2), 335–338.

National Association of Social Workers. (2000). *Code of ethics of the National Association of Social Workers.* Washington, DC: NASW Press.

National Association of Social Workers. (2010). *Standards for cultural competence in social work practice.* Washington, DC: NASW.

Williams, D. R. & Jackson, P. B. (2005). Social sources of racial disparities in health. *Health Affairs, 24*(2), 325–334.

AT-RISK COMMUNITIES: EXAMINING POVERTY

6

LEARNING OBJECTIVES

This chapter focuses on helping students learn the key components of poverty in the United States. After reading this chapter, the reader will be able to

- identify key features of poverty,
- identify existing inequalities that contribute to poverty, and
- identify the roles social workers play in combating poverty.

WHAT IS POVERTY?

Though everyone may have a different definition of what is to be poor, particularly poverty in other countries, the question is what constitutes someone living in America as poor? Poverty in the United States today is measured in two ways: by the national poverty guidelines and by the national poverty thresholds (U.S. Census Bureau, 2010). The U.S. Census Bureau's (2010) definition of poverty is defined by a set of thresholds developed in the 1960s; a family is considered living in poverty if their income is lower than the official poverty threshold. This measure is calculated by comparing a family's or individual's resources to a threshold, which differs by family size and is calculated to represent the minimum income needed to live at a basic level.

The Census Bureau applies the national poverty thresholds to determine the number of individuals living in poverty across the United States. According to the 2015 Census report, 15.5 million children were living in poverty in the United States. Families composed of four people, making less than $22,050 a year qualified as poor (impoverished) in 2009, per the federal guidelines (U.S. Census Bureau, 2010). These poverty guidelines serve as the baseline for eligibility criteria for federal assistance for Medicaid, Head Start, and the Supplemental Nutrition and Assistance Program.

DEFINITIONS OF POVERTY

Absolute poverty is defined by persistent poverty and deprivation of basic needs, and is the most common form of poverty measurement in the U.S. (Kopezyska-Sikorska & Szysko, 2001).

Relative poverty is defined as the lack of financial means combined with other factors, such as cost of and standard of living (Iceland, 2005; Kopezyska-Sikorska & Szysko, 2001).

Subjective poverty is defined as when an individual perceives their income level as being insufficient (Kopezyska-Sikorska & Szyszko, 2001).

CHILDREN LIVING IN POVERTY

The population of the United States is roughly 318.9 million people (U.S. Census Bureau 2014); 73 million are children, of which, 15.5 million live below the federal poverty line. Children aged birth through age four are the largest proportion of U.S. children living in poverty, with 9 million, or 43%, living below federal poverty baseline. Poverty rates of children under the age of 18 in the United States are historically among the highest of any other industrialized nation. Canada (14%) and the United Kingdom (7.8%) both have significantly lower child poverty rates than the United States (Chen & Corak, 2008).

RISK FACTORS ASSOCIATED WITH LIVING IN POVERTY

Children living in poverty are at a higher risk for social, emotional, and behavioral problems. Children living in poverty must contend with dilapidated schools and unsafe living conditions. In addition, these children typically live in unsafe neighborhoods, which have an increased rate of crime and violence, with an increased exposure to drugs. Children experiencing poverty in early childhood (birth to age 5) are at a greater risk for future poor health. Duncan, Kalil and Ziol-Guest (2010) found that children who are poor at a younger age are two times more likely to suffer poor overall health and elevated stress levels as adults than children who do not experience poverty. Parents under stress due to living in poverty argue more than those not in poverty, therefore impacting the quality of a nurturing environment. The four primary risk factors affecting families living in poverty are: (a) emotional and social challenges, (b) acute and chronic stressors, (c) delays in cognitive development, and (d) health and safety issues. Common presenting problems in low-income families include chemical dependence, depression, and hectic, sometimes uncertain work schedules. Factors that negatively impact healthy attachments hinder children's interpersonal and cognitive development.

POVERTY IN DIFFERENT NEIGHBORHOODS

Poverty is widespread throughout the United States, although two out of every three children living below the poverty line live in southern or western regions of the country. In the Northeast and Midwest families living in poverty are concentrated in urban areas, whereas in the South and West, families are concentrated in rural communities (U.S. Census Bureau, 2010). Below, we present a breakdown of poverty by neighborhood types.

URBAN NEIGHBORHOODS

Of all children living in poverty, 75% of them live in urban neighborhoods, hence increasing the likelihood of attending failing schools and living in violent neighborhoods, as compared to their peers (Buddin & Zamarro, 2009; Kiser, 2007).

SUBURBAN NEIGHBORHOODS

Historically, suburban communities have typically and visually been exempt from poverty, yet there have been changes in the last few years. Over 29% of residents dwelling in suburban neighborhoods are currently living in poverty (Holliday & Dwyer, 2009).

RURAL NEIGHBORHOODS

There is a higher overall population of rural residents living in poverty than urban residents. Of rural dwellers, 13.4% live in poverty (Dayton, 2003). Individuals living in rural poverty are less likely to take advantage of federal aid, such as welfare, and instead work hard to obtain a high moral standing in their communities (Sherman, 2006).

Improving impoverished neighborhoods may be the key to poverty alleviation, as research shows that living in neighborhoods with a high concentration of poverty can lead to both physical and emotional consequences.

THE "WAR ON POVERTY"

President Lyndon B. Johnson initiated the War on Poverty in 1964. His War on Poverty introduced initiatives designed to improve the education, health, skills, jobs, and access to economic resources of those living in poverty. These initiatives prevented millions of hardworking Americans from slipping into poverty during the worst economic crisis since the Great Depression. Poverty has declined by more than one third since 1967.

In 2012, there were 49.7 million Americans struggling with the economic and social sufferings of living below the poverty line, including 13.4 million children. Programs designed to assist with economic security assisted over 45 million people in poverty in 2012, and helped an average of 27 million people out of poverty per year for 45 years between 1968 and 2012.

The programs listed below are examples of federal assistance available to aid those living in poverty or with low socioeconomic status.

SOCIAL SECURITY BENEFITS

Social Security plays a crucial role in lowering poverty among the elderly. Poverty among those aged 65 and older was 35% in 1960. Following rapid expansions in Social Security in the 1960s and 1970s, poverty among the elderly fell to 14.8% in 2012.

Social Security benefits reduced the 2012 poverty rate by 8.5% among all individuals, and by 39.9% among those aged 65 or older (Social Security Administration, 2014).

THE TEMPORARY ASSISTANCE FOR NEEDY FAMILIES (TANF)

The Temporary Assistance for Needy Families (TANF) program is designed to help families achieve self-sufficiency. TANF assists families living in poverty who have children under the age of 18 by providing funds to help sustain families while they are struggling to find employment. States receive block grants to (a) provide assistance to needy families so that children can be cared for in their own homes, (b) reduce dependency by promoting job preparation, work, and marriage, (c) prevent and reduce the incidence of pregnancies out-of-wedlock, and (d) encourage the formation and maintenance of two-parent families.

THE SUPPLEMENTAL NUTRITION ASSISTANCE PROGRAM (SNAP)

The Supplemental Nutrition Assistance Program (SNAP), formerly known as the Food Stamp Program, reduced poverty in 2012 by 1.6% among all individuals, and by 3.0% among children. SNAP offers nutrition assistance to millions of eligible, low-income individuals and families and provides economic benefits to communities. SNAP is the largest program in the domestic hunger safety net.

HEAD START

President Johnson enacted the Head Start program, which was designed as an early intervention for children living in poverty. Head Start's purpose was to raise academic and social competence of students living below the poverty line. For children from low-income families under the age of 5 years, it promotes school readiness through education, health, social, and other services. Head Start and other high-quality preschool programs include higher educational attainment, employment, and earnings, and lower rates of teen pregnancy and crime.

EDUCATION

President Obama has advanced reforms of the nation's K-12 education system to support higher standards that attempt to prepare students to succeed in college and the workplace; and encouraged a national effort to turn around our lowest-achieving schools.

WHO ARE THE POOR?

The following table identifies at-risk groups in the United States that have a higher likelihood of living in poverty (U.S. Census Bureau, 2010).

Fig 6.1

Poverty Rates by Characteristics

Source: U.S. Census Bureau (2012). Copyright in the Public Domain.

2012 POVERTY RATES BY CERTAIN CHARACTERISTICS	
INDIVIDUAL CHARACTERISTICS	**SUPPLEMENTAL POVERTY MEASURE BY PERCENTAGES**
Less than High School (age 25–64)	25.3
High School (age 25–64)	17.5
College (age 25–64)	5.9
Female	16.7
African American	25.8
Hispanic	27.8
Asian	16.7
Native Alaskans/American Indian	30.3
White	10.7

PERCEPTIONS OF POVERTY

In 1961 Oscar Lewis wrote the book *The Children of Sanchez,* which created the term *culture of poverty* initially reinforcing the myth and perception among Americans that there is an underlying culture of poverty shared by low-income communities. Lewis ethnographically studied small Mexican communities living in poverty and generalized his findings into a list of 50 common qualities shared by these individuals. The list included qualities such as a lack of future planning, a lack of common history, and increased violent behavior. As stated in previous chapters of this textbook, American society has historically regarded poverty as an individual problem (Lewis, 1961). Many upper- and middle-class individuals believe that those living in poverty lack work ethic, are unmotivated, and are not good parents. Those individuals living in poverty may believe there is a stigma regarding their financial situation. Furthermore, they may believe some of the tenets of the culture of poverty, leading to confrontational actions or social withdrawal. These societal perceptions of blaming the victims lead to fewer social and employment opportunities.

AT-RISK GROUPS

- Women, who are overrepresented among the poor, especially single heads of households
- Racial minorities, who often have fewer opportunities for access to education and face economic discrimination
- Those who have not completed high school
- Children, one quarter of the population, but over a third of those living in poverty
- Older adults 9% of whom live below the poverty line
- The physically or mentally disabled

CHAPTER EXERCISES

1. What is the definition of poverty and how does it differ from your own personal definition?

2. What factors cause poverty?

3. Discuss some of the consequences of children living in poverty.

REFERENCES

Buddin, R. & Zamarro, G. (2009). Teacher qualifications and student achievement in urban elementary schools. *Journal of Urban Economics, 66*, 103–115.

Chen, W-H. & Corak, M. (2008). Child poverty and changes in child poverty. *Demography, 45*(3), 537–553.

Dayton, J. (2003). Rural children, rural schools, and public school funding litigation: A real problem in search of a real solution. *Nebraska Law Review, 82* (99) 1–7.

Duncan, G. J., Ziol-Guest, K. M., Kalil, A. (2010). Early-childhood poverty and adult attainment, behavior, and health. *Child Development, 81*(1), 306–325.

Holliday, A. L. & Dwyer, R. E. (2009). Suburban neighborhood poverty in U.S. metropolitan areas in 2000. *City & Community, 8*(2), 155–176.

Iceland, J. (2005). Measuring poverty: Theoretical and empirical considerations. *Measurement: Interdisciplinary Research and Perspectives, 3*(4), 199–235.

Kiser, L. J. (2007). Protecting children from the dangers of urban poverty. *Clinical Psychology Review, 27*, 211–225.

Kopezyska-Sikorska, J. & Szyszko, M. (2001). Poverty: Comparing perceptions and understanding among school and preschool aged children. *International Journal of Early Childhood, 33*(1), 19–25.

Lewis, O. (1961). *The children of Sanchez: Autobiography of a Mexican family.* New York: Random House.

Sherman, J. (2006). Coping with rural poverty: Economic survival and moral capital in rural America. *Social Forces, 85*(2), 891–913.

Social Security Administration. (2014). Contribution and benefit base. Retrieved from http://www.ssa.gov/oact/cola/cbb.html

U.S. Census Report. (2011). Income, Poverty, and Health Insurance Coverage in the United States: 2011. Retrieved from https://www.census.gov

U.S. Census Bureau. (2010). Poverty. Retrieved from: http://www.census.gov

PART 4

SERVING VARIOUS CLIENT POPULATIONS

7

PRACTICE SETTINGS AND FIELDS OF SOCIAL WORK

LEARNING OBJECTIVES

This chapter focuses on examining main fields of social work practice. After reading this chapter, the reader will be able to

- identify different opportunities for fields of practice for social workers,
- identify different practice settings where social workers are employed, and
- identify and classify the different roles in which social workers function with respect to individuals, groups and communities.

INTRODUCTION

The social work profession offers one of the most comprehensive ranges of settings and opportunities for the professional. Social workers work with individuals, families, and communities. According to the U.S. Bureau of Labor Statistics Occupational Outlook Handbook for 2012–13 the job outlook for social workers is positive due to a projected increase in demand for health care and social services. Employment predictions for professionals in this field are expected to rise 25 percent by the year 2020. Social workers are found in public agencies, private businesses, hospitals, clinics, schools, nursing homes, private practices, police departments, courts, and countless other interesting workplaces. Social workers can be managers, supervisors, and administrators in a variety of settings. There are three levels of practice for social workers: the micro, mezzo, or macro level.

MICRO PRACTICE

Micro or clinical social work encompasses working directly with individuals, families, groups, and communities to help bring about social, emotional, and behavioral change. This level of social work practitioners is the largest group of mental health providers in the United States. Clinical social workers at this level have opportunities to work in a wide variety of settings, including private practice, schools, hospitals, and substance abuse treatment centers. Micro, or clinical social workers must possess an understanding of human development, relational and group processes, cultural differences, and social policies. Job duties can involve, but are not limited to

- diagnosing and treating mental, behavioral, and emotional disorders;
- collaborating with clients and other health care professionals on treatment strategies;
- providing group, family, or couples therapy; and
- developing and implementing treatment plans.

MEZZO PRACTICE

Mezzo social work involves working with small to medium-sized groups or organizations in settings such as schools, community service organizations, or businesses, to promote cultural or institutional change.

As a mezzo social worker, job duties may involve

- providing group therapy or counseling to support groups or community organizations;
- facilitating group discussions or processes to improve decision making or strengthen relationships within a team, business, or community group;
- organizing community groups or leading human services programs or agencies; and
- evaluating a social service agency's goals, structures, and operations to improve its client services.

MACRO PRACTICE

Macro social work involves working on large-scale systems aiming to promote change at the organizational, community, societal, or global level.

Macro social workers may have duties that include:

- Leading nonprofit organizations or human services programs at the local, state, national, or international level;
- Organizing communities to identify and address community-based issues or build community capacity; and
- Advocating for change to public policies that affect entire communities or populations, or conducting research to inform those changes.

The core body of knowledge of the social work profession identifies concerns and challenges in the client's environment, taking a person-in-environment perspective. Social work involves skills, techniques, and methods to provide professional support for clients, including removing barriers to service delivery, while maintaining ethical integrity and respect for the client's autonomy. One of the core values of the social work profession is adhering to the person-in-environment perspective, which suggests considering interventions that speak to various aspects of a client's life. As discussed previously in Chapter 1 of this textbook, intervention strategies range from individual counseling, to family therapy, to community advocacy.

Regardless of level of client involvement, client population, or practice setting social workers are employed in, they should possess the key characteristics listed in Figure 7.1.

Fig 7.1

Key Aspects of the Social Work Profession

- Social workers must possess a basic understanding of different client systems, within the framework of the client's culture and community, as a main link for self-definition, growth and change, and the environmental forces that affect a client's potential for growth and change.

- Social workers must have a thorough understanding of the profession's values, roles, and ethics related to the services provided to the clientele.

- Possessing knowledge of the importance of the worker-client relationship, and skill in establishing mutually respectful, empowerment is essential for the social worker-client relationship.

- Ability in basic interviewing skills is essential. Listening, empathy, genuineness, pacing, confrontation, and focusing are key skills that the professional must hone in on regardless of the client population or setting.

- Within the biopsychosocial perspective of social work, it is necessary to have the skills to assess the client strengths and problems, and the ability to recognize the influence of gender, race, socioeconomic status, sexual orientation, and the influence of social and political environments in the client's well-being within the viewpoint of a biopsychosocial perspective is necessary.

- Social workers must create and discuss mutually agreed upon goals with clients. Goals are always created with the client. The creation and discussion of mutually-agreed upon goals with clients, and developing appropriate service plans from these goals is needed.

- Knowledge of, and beginning skill in a range of social work roles, including case management, interventions with different client systems, and crisis intervention.

- Knowledge of, and beginning skill in the monitoring and evaluation of practice, and of the importance of involving clients in this evaluative process.

- Knowledge of, and beginning skill in appropriate termination strategies with clients.

- The capacity for critical self-awareness and self-examination and the effective use of supervision, feedback from colleagues, and current social work research and literature.

SPECIALIZED AREAS IN SOCIAL WORK PRACTICE

Social work is an extensive professional field that encompasses several chief areas of work and/or specialization. Some social workers who have advanced degrees (an MSW or a PhD) develop specialized skills. Social workers may specialize in treating specific problems such as mental illnesses, child behavioral problems, child welfare, probation, substance abuse, marriage (or more generally, couples) problems, domestic violence, or living with chronic illnesses such as cancer and HIV/AIDS. Social workers can also specialize in working with a particular age group, such as children and adolescents, or in aging, referred to as gerontology. Some social workers focus on short-term therapy or on crisis intervention, such as in emergency preparedness and disaster relief, conflict resolution and mediation, or violence and victim services.

The main areas of social work practice are listed below:

- **Social casework (case management)** is a method of helping through a relationship that taps personal and other resources for coping with problems. Interviewing and assessment are major tools of casework. Assessing the client's needs to address any social, psychological, physical or mental health, or economic problems, with community agency resources and/or public welfare programs is the key goal. Social workers help clients become eligible for a variety of services designed to improve their economic, social and/or health functioning. Providing case work involves providing social, health and/or public welfare services through public, private, and community organizations and agencies.

- **School social workers** work in school settings, typically 1st–12th grade to help students who are experiencing emotional, social and/or economic problems, overcome them and assist them with focusing on academics. In this setting social workers address the students' presenting problems, typically using a systems approach to identify health (physical, mental) family, or environmental problems that are negatively impacting the student.

- **Children and families:** Unfortunately due to multiple socioeconomic factors facing many children and families, there is an increasing demand for child and family social workers. More than 15 million children (22%) live in poverty. With respect to children in the foster care system, over 20,000 young adults age out of foster care each year without sufficient housing or financial assistance (National Center for Child Poverty, 2014).

- **Clinical social workers** can have private practices, and work in mental health or psychiatric settings (in-patient or out-patient), where they administer psychotherapy and counseling. They may also work with employee assistance programs within larger companies that have numerous employees. Clinical social workers provide an array of mental health services, including assessment, diagnosis, and treatment, and use a variety of psychotherapeutic theories and tools with individuals, couples, families, and groups.

Clinical social workers comprise the largest percentage of mental health service providers in the United States. According to the Bureau of Labor Statistics, mental health services will grow by 12% between 2014 and 2024.

- **In mental health** settings, social workers assess, diagnose, and implement services for clients diagnosed with a mental health disorder. These services can be administered in in-patient or out-patient settings. According to the National Institute of Mental Health, approximately 57.7 million Americans (one in four) will experience a mental disorder in their life time and with legislation requiring health plans cover these services, social workers in this area are in great demand.

- **Medical social workers** work with patients and families in hospitals, long term care facilities, short-term care facilities, outpatient offices, hospice programs, rehabilitation programs, and other health settings to assist with difficulties that accompany illness, such as economic need, disability, and lack of resources. Social workers may find a lot of job opportunities in these settings as institutions attempt to meet accountability standards mandated by the implementation of the Affordable Care Act (ACA). Due to the ACA, 32 million previously uninsured Americans gained access to health care, increasing the demand for social workers in hospitals and health clinics (Namrata, Finegold, & Gee, 2016). When working in a hospital setting, medical social workers coordinate services for home care and equipment following discharge, or for referral to rehabilitation and long-term care facilities.

- **In administration and management**, social workers manage programs and systems, and employ other social workers who provide direct services to individuals, families, and groups for social, health, and public welfare services. In this setting the social worker manages delivery of public and private social and health service programs, and evaluate the programs' effectiveness in order to improve services.

- **Crisis intervention** involves emergency psychological care in crisis situations to help clients restore mental state equilibrium and minimize the potential for psychological trauma. Trauma treatment involves restoring a sense of safety and ensuring that social services do not inadvertently re-traumatize clients. Sixty percent of adults experienced trauma or violence in childhood, and 26% of children in the U.S. will witness or experience violence before they are 4 years old (National Center for Mental Health Promotion and Youth Violence Prevention, 2012).

- **Community organization** social workers work in collaboration with private, governmental, or community groups to recognize needs and to create or improve services to meet those needs. They work to improve systems and develop new resources to provide more people in the community with access to the services they need to function at their best.

- **In social policy and research**, social workers analyze social problems, and design and conduct research studies to find ways to overcome those problems. Social work researchers measure the effectiveness of social programs, interventions, assessments and agency operations, and analyze the results to recommend ways to improve treatments or solutions. With respect to social policy, social workers may conduct research projects to determine how to address social issues, such as homelessness, substance abuse, poverty, and child welfare services. After in-depth analysis of the policies or presenting problems, social workers plan and implement interventions, work on revising or creating new policies, and advocate to reform social conditions.

EDUCATION NEEDED TO BECOME A SOCIAL WORKER

Most social work positions require that candidates have the training and expertise that is derived from a four-year social work program, culminating in a Bachelor of Social Work degree (BSW). For some advanced positions, employers look for candidates with a Master of Social Work (MSW) degree.

BACHELOR OF SOCIAL WORK (BSW)

A Bachelor of Social Work degree (BSW) is required for most entry-level positions in this field. To be identified as a social worker, the professional must have at least a BSW; others who work in the field providing case management are called caseworkers. BSW degree programs teach students about human behavior, cultural competency, and policies pertaining to social welfare. Social workers who have BSW's are generalist practitioners, meaning they do not have a specialization. Most are employed in direct practice settings with individuals, families, and groups and provide basic counseling and case management. In addition, these professionals can facilitate group counseling and link clients with community resources or public welfare programs.

MASTER OF SOCIAL WORK (MSW)

A master's degree is often mandatory for social work jobs in some settings, such as schools or healthcare facilities. It is crucial that one attends an MSW program that is accredited by the Council on Social Work Education (CSWE); if the school is not accredited, employers will not consider the degree and the student cannot take any licensure exams. In most cases, a Master of Social Work Degree (MSW) takes one year of full time attendance if the student already holds a BSW; this is called advanced standing. If the student does not have a BSW, but has a bachelor's degree in a related field, i.e., psychology or sociology, then the program typically takes two years of full time attendance. MSW programs train students for employment in an area of specialization and help them develop advanced skills to serve a large number of clients, do clinical assessments, and provide supervision. All MSW programs and most BSW programs require students to complete supervised fieldwork.

PH.D. IN SOCIAL WORK

An MSW is typically required in order for one to pursue a Ph.D. in social work. The Ph.D. prepares individuals for careers as researchers, scholars and educators. Doctoral students choose from different concentrations (i.e., advanced practice, social policy or analysis, or administration). A Ph.D. candidate takes approximately two years of full-time coursework. They master content in social work methods, related behavioral or social sciences, substantive fields of practice, and prepare and defend a dissertation. Graduates typically seek advanced careers in research or academia. This degree allows the individual to expand their capacities to conceptualize, develop, evaluate, and disseminate knowledge of the problems that impact the human condition and analyze or develop strategies aimed to change those conditions. Education on this level allows one to attain and develop a critical understanding of the different systems and forces that shape the human experience and social work practice as a whole.

DOCTOR OF SOCIAL WORK (DSW)

The Doctor of Social Work or DSW is considered a practice doctorate degree. This degree gives the professional the opportunity to conduct practical research and lead social service programs (e.g. Director of Social Work). A Ph.D. degree is considered to be more research-than clinically-oriented, and typically focuses on educational practices.

SALARIES FOR SOCIAL WORKERS

Salaries for social workers vary greatly and depend on a few factors: (a) level of education attained, (b) licensures attained, (c) state where presently employed, and (d) employment setting. According to NASW Workforce Study Group a strong, positive correlation exists between education level and compensation for social work practitioners. According to the NASW, the median base pay for social workers with a bachelor's degree is approximately $40,000; for MSWs, the median base wage is $55,000 and for a social worker with a Ph.D. or a Doctorate of Social Work (DSW) the median pay is approximately $72,000; please be mindful that these are approximate salaries and of course can range greatly due to location, setting, and other factors mentioned above.

RANGE OF SALARY BY JOB CATEGORY

According to a 2014 Bureau of Labor Statistics report, salaries for social workers in the field's major categories are the following:

- **Child, school, and family social workers** earn about $44,410 annually.
- **Healthcare social workers** earn an average wage of $50,500.
- **Mental health and substance abuse social workers** earn an average of $42,650.

CHAPTER EXERCISES

1. Describe the different settings where a social worker can find employment;

2. Analyze the differences between micro, mezzo, and macro practice; and

3. Discuss the different types of degrees available in the study of social work.

REFERENCES

Bureau of Labor Statistics. (2014). *Social workers. Occupational Outlook Handbook, 2012–13 edition.* Retrieved from httphttps://www.bls.gov/ooh/

National Center for Children in Poverty. (2014). *Basic facts about low-income children fact sheet.* Columbia University, Mailman School of Public Health.

National Center for Mental Health Promotion and Youth Violence Prevention. (2012). *Childhood Trauma and Its Effect on Healthy Development.* Retrieved from http://sshs.promoteprevent.org/sites/default/files/trauma_brief_in_final.pdf

Uberoi, N., Finegold, K., and Gee, E. (2016). Health Insurance Coverage and the Affordable Care Act, 2010–2016. Department of Health and Human Services: Office of the Assistant Secretary for Planning and Evaluation, 2016.

8 WORKING WITH INDIVIDUALS

LEARNING OBJECTIVES

This chapter focuses on social work practice with individuals. Social work with individuals is one of the main aspects of a generalist approach to social work practice. After reading this chapter, the reader will be able to

- identify the history of social work practice with individuals, and
- identify a variety of skills social workers use with clients.

This chapter examines the foundation of social work practice with individuals. Working with individuals is referred to as micro social work practice; typically this is the primary focus of most practicing social workers, where the main emphasis is to help individuals help themselves.

Direct practice with individuals at the micro level is a diverse route of practice guided by the problem-solving process, along with the core values of the profession including sensitivity and attention to social and economic justice. When working with clients, social workers must be knowledgeable about when concrete services are needed (food, shelter, clothing, and other social services) in an effort to enhance the quality of life for the individual. Even though the social worker's client is an individual, the professional is aware that people do not operate in a vacuum and recognizes the external factors and systems that impact the client and their presenting problem(s). Social workers must be able to select the appropriate intervention and know when and how to implement various theories. Social work with individuals is one of the main parts of a generalist approach to social work practice. Two main components addressed with the client are socialization and re-socialization. Socialization involves identity and skill development, while re-socialization may include social control and rehabilitation services and activities.

HISTORY OF SOCIAL WORK PRACTICE WITH INDIVIDUALS

As examined in Chapter 2 of this textbook, the history of social work began initially with the Charity Organizations Society (COS), the friendly visitors, and outdoor relief, working with individuals and families (Richmond, 1922). Using the medical profession as a model, Mary Richmond, in her 1917 book, *Social Diagnosis,* presented a model of social diagnosis as a technique for friendly visitors to gather information and conduct assessments of those in need.

Today, this is the model for casework. In addition, Richmond's 1922 book, *What Is Social Case Work?* provides a foundation for teaching and practice of social casework.

Though the ideologies of the profession have changed from the perception of early caseworkers, who were trained to help individuals resolve problems caused by "deviations from accepted standards of normal social life," to recognizing the external factors like social and economic injustice, racism, sexism, oppression, poverty, etc. that impact the client's life (Dolgoff, Feldstein & Skolnik, 1993). This shift of ideologies to incorporating a more holistic perspective began in the 1960s. The use of the generalist model emphasized an ecological, systemic, strengths-based approach for the social worker.

The following is a partial list of presenting issues where social workers help clients:

- Beginning or ending a phase of life, such as marriage, divorce, parenting, career change, caring for a family member, retirement, grief, etc.
- Relationship difficulties—friendship, family, marital, parent/child, or employment.
- Life crises such as physical or mental health problems, violence, natural or economic disasters, and legal problems.
- Chemical dependency and addictions, such as alcohol, drugs, food, gambling, sexual, or spending.

INTRODUCTIONS

Because first impressions are so important in any encounter, the first face-to-face meeting can impact all future encounters between a client and social worker. An effective beginning results when the worker and the prospective client accomplish the purpose for which they first meet (e.g., information gathering, information giving, assessment forming, or change making) and reach a mutual agreement concerning a next step in the process.

When first meeting a client, introduce yourself by your full name and profession:

> "Hi, my name is Bianca Smith, and I am an intake social worker here on the adolescent mental health unit. I have been working here for the past 3 years, and I work with teens like yourself who have different situations they want to talk about and work on."

A pleasant facial expression and a handshake are generally appropriate, but the social worker must be mindful of cultural differences and age appropriate behavior. I would not necessarily shake a 6 year old's hand, unless they reached out to shake mine. Perhaps a fist bump may be more appropriate, but never a kiss ANYWHERE or a hug on the first encounter. Being culturally competent is key in the beginning phase, (i.e., it would be inappropriate for a female social worker to shake hands with a client who is a Hasidic Jew). In an effort to be culturally competent, ask clients how they wish to be addressed and how to pronounce their names.

BEGINNING

When first meeting a client, the worker needs skills in each of the following areas:

- Introducing yourself without being arrogant: please see above paragraph for example;
- Seeking an introduction from the client: a common question is "Tell me about yourself";
- Describing an initial purpose: inform the client about how the session will proceed and the types of services you or your agency provide. Clients that have never sought social services may tend to look to the social worker for leadership. The social worker can discuss their view of the purpose for the session in an effort to provide guidance for the client, which may reduce any stress a client may have about the meeting. The key skill of "starting where the client is," i.e., letting the client begin where they want to without the social worker imposing a specific agenda for the session) assists the social worker in gaining an understanding of the client's perception of the problem and their desired goals.
- Discussing issues that impact confidentiality: In social work there is no such thing as absolute confidentiality; there are three scenarios in which social workers must break confidentiality:

  - abuse (child, elder, etc.)

  - suicide

  - homicide

When the purpose of the meeting is clear, workers may then describe the roles they will assume in the helping process. As listed in Chapter 1 of this textbook, possible roles include

- advocate,
- educator,

- facilitator,
- investigator,
- counselor,
- mediator,
- therapist,
- case manager, and
- broker.

The following practice theories are typically utilized when working with individuals (Healy, 2005):

- ecological/systems framework,
- ego psychology,
- problem solving approach,
- cognitive behavioral approaches,
- reality therapy,
- task-centered method,
- client-centered therapy,
- feminist therapy, and
- solution-focused therapy.

PLANNED CHANGE PROCESS

Social workers take specific and deliberate steps to encourage and facilitate movement towards change for a client. The primary goal in working with the client is to promote and support social functioning of the client. Social functioning includes the capacity, motivation, and resources to meet basic human needs and carry out social roles (child, parent, student, employee, citizen, spouse, etc.). All interventions revolve around the *planned change process*. The planned change process is where the social worker and client work together to strategize and implement a series of activities aimed at enhancing the client's functioning and well-being. The planned change process involves the development and implementation of an approach for improving or altering patterns of behavior, an environment, or other setting(s).

Planned change process in generalist social work practice for interventions with individuals, families, groups, organizations, and communities consists of four phases:

- engagement,
- assessment,
- intervention, and
- evaluation

ENGAGEMENT

Engaging the client is the first step in building a successful relationship for the social worker. It's like the adage says, "the first impression is the most important". Not properly engaging clients can result in unsuccessful experiences for all involved. This process sets the tone for the relationship of clients and social workers and impacts future work. In addition, the process elicits information in an open and trusting manner using both verbal and nonverbal communication. Trust and respect are two key components of building a healthy therapeutic relationship. By using and recognizing verbal and nonverbal communication, social workers establish rapport and respect. Rapport is the client's perception that she or he has established a congenial relationship with the social worker that promotes a sense of trust, where the client feels comfortable sharing personal information; sometimes information that may have never been revealed to anyone before.

VERBAL COMMUNICATION

When attempting to engage the client and build rapport, the social worker must attend to the following aspects of verbal communication:

- Listen to the client without interrupting or interjecting words.
- Speak with language that demonstrates empathy and warmth.
- Use language respectful to the client's culture, ethnicity, and social group.
- Utilize verbiage suitable to client's educational level.
- Do NOT use professional jargon. We should not expect clients to know our professional language, plus it can make clients believe you are attempting to prove that you are smarter than they are.
- Speak at a pace and volume that the client can hear and follow.

Nonverbal communication can be more important than verbal communication as it is believed that human beings pay more attention to it than to verbal communication. That being said, the social worker must always be cognizant of their verbal communication, a task that many individuals find hard at times.

NONVERBAL COMMUNICATION

Essential nonverbal communication skills to be aware of and adhere to are listed below:

- You should directly face the client and be at the same level when sitting, i.e., the social worker's chair should be at the same height as the client's chair.

- Maintain eye contact when culturally appropriate.
- Use nonverbal gestures such as a nod of the head or a lean of the face and other appropriate facial expressions that indicate interest, warmth, and empathy.
- Maintain focus on the client; do not think ahead about your next question or comment.
- Facial expressions must be congruent with your responses.
- Avoid distracting behaviors (e.g., tapping your pen or pencil, playing with your hair, etc.).

ASSESSMENT

The second stage of the planned change process is assessment. The assessment phase involves gathering, analyzing and synthesizing information about the client, as well as recognizing the client's needs and strengths. This summary are discussed with the client. In the assessment phase, the social worker uses theoretical frameworks to better understand the client's situation and plan an appropriate intervention. In an effort to conduct a proper and thorough assessment, the social worker's first task—to establish a therapeutic relationship with rapport, trust, and respect—is utilized in this phase as well. Rapport and trust is still a main priority for the social worker so that the assessment phase is successful. If wrong information is provided by the client, either due to mistrust or telling half truths (i.e., pertinent information is withheld from the social worker), there is a trickle down effect in the theoretical framework and interventions that are used by the social worker.

After gathering relevant information about the client and selecting an appropriate theoretical framework, the next step in the assessment process is for the social worker to consider the types and quality of questions to ask the client. It is pertinent for the social worker to ask only questions that will better assist the client; questions should never be asked due to sole curiosity. A common question that a social worker may want to ask a client who is HIV+ is "How did you acquire the disease?" This question is of course important to ask if conducting a bio-psychosocial assessment, but if the goals of the services are for housing, then this question is irrelevant. There must be a mutual agreement between the social worker and the client during the assessment phase for the assessment to be successful. Social workers must not impose their goals on the client; the goals created must be mutual.

Two key components of the assessment phase are planning and implementation.

Planning involves establishing the goals, corresponding objectives, and changes expected. Some important questions that must be examined are

- How does the client prioritize presenting issues in her or his life?
- Are there any ethical or legal issues that must be addressed before action can take place?
- Are the plan's outcomes reasonable and measurable?
- Is the plan based on a theoretical model or perspective?

Implementation involves taking action with respect to the intervention, based on the plan. The implementation is based on a practice model or perspective (i.e., generalist, strengths, ecological models and practice theories and approaches).

The social worker's understanding and interpretation of the information collected during the first phase, the engagement phase, sets the foundation for planning and implementation. Deciding on what needs to change, what resources are available, and the strengths of the client are critical in this stage.

To use the strengths-based perspective properly, social workers must consistently compare the client's goals with their own to ensure that the goals being worked toward are the client's and not the social worker's. Motivation for change is likely to be higher when the goal is one in which we are invested. The social worker does not have to agree with the goals of the client, but must respect them. In addition, the agreed upon goals must correspond with the client's needs and the availability of services. Again, questions should be focused on gathering only information relevant to the situation at hand.

In the assessment phase, the social worker does the following key activities:

- identifies client needs and issues;
- identifies client strengths and resources; and
- prioritizes needs and desired outcomes.

INTERVENTION

The third stage of the planned change process is the intervention phase. In the intervention phase, actual work is completed; both the client and the social worker follow the agreed upon plan to achieve the agreed upon goals. Building on information gathered in the assessment phase, the social worker focuses on prioritizing the client's needs and mobilizing the client's resources and strengths to enable the desired change during the intervention phase. In addition, both parties identify barriers to goal attainment and discuss and evaluate strategies to overcome them.

Devising a measurable goal for attaining the stated goals is essential. A measurable goal is necessary so the social worker and client know that the goal has been accomplished. Therefore making a goal quantifiable is key. For example, a student saying "I want to improve my grades" is not measurable, because the definition of *improve* is subjective. How does the social worker know when this goal is accomplished if the client has not said how she or he plans to measure this goal? A quantifiable goal is one that is measurable: "I want to raise my GPA by one point." With this goal, if the client's GPA is 2.5 and then it is raised to 3.5, we know the goal was accomplished because the GPA was raised by the stated goal of one point.

- Implement plan. Periodically, the social worker monitors the intervention to determine if adjustments or further assessments are needed.

This must be done because we want know that life is not stagnant and it does not happen in a bubble. We must monitor interventions to ensure that goals can be met in the stated time period to ensure that clients are not setting themselves up for failure. It is always important to create short term and long terms goals. The idea here is once a short term goal is achieved, this increases the client's self-esteem and motivation to accomplish longer term goal(s).

Key features of the intervention phase include

- This phase can be a time of gratification and fulfillment, but frustration and struggle can also ensue if the client does not have a strong support system or various barriers to the goal arise, delaying achievement of the goal (in the eyes of the client).
- Changing lifelong behaviors and patterns of interaction can be tough even when change is desired (old habits are hard to break).
- When goals are mutually agreed upon by both the social worker and the client, the intervention can produce positive outcomes.

EVALUATION

The fourth and final stage of the planed change process is the evaluation phase. In this phase, the social worker and client assess progress and success of the planned change effort and determine if it is time to terminate the relationship. The assessment and intervention phases must have been conducted in a comprehensive and collaborative manner; social work is not done to the client but rather it is done with the client. Both of these phases can be accomplished effectively only if the goals were agreed upon mutually and the accompanying objectives were measurable and specific.

Key features of the evaluation phase include:

- determine if goals were appropriate and achievable;
- determine if goals were achieved, examine the reasons goals were or were not achieved; and
- determine if the intervention used was appropriate.

Termination occurs when goals have been attained, the client or social worker ends the intervention, or the goals are changed. Terminating the intervention once goals and objectives have been reached and evaluating the change process is an important process for the social worker to learn for future practice. Evaluate specific procedures and techniques used or which should be used to bring the professional relationship to a close and terminate the helping process. Develop a plan with the client for maintenance or follow-up. Termination, defined as the official ending of the social worker-client relationship, is the goal from the very first encounter. Failure to establish termination as the eventual goal can lead to the client becoming dependent on the social worker. The length and number of the sessions should be stated during the first session with the client; this is referred to as *contracting*.

The social work relationship can be terminated if the following occurs:

- The goals have been successfully achieved.
- The client stops treatment because he or she no longer agrees with the goals and plans.
- The client is no longer eligible to receive social services.
- Social worker feels that goals cannot be achieved or the client is unwilling to comply with the contract.
- The social worker or agency is no longer the most appropriate service provider for the client.

Key features of the evaluation phase include termination and follow-up. The social worker devises a plan for maintaining the goals accomplished. It is essential for social workers to remind clients of their strengths and the resources used so that they can tap into them when a future problem arises and feel empowered to work and confront future problems. Communicate to the client that if future events create a real need for assistance, services can be resumed.

Fig 8.1

Four Phases of the Planned Change Process

Engagement	• Substantively and effectively prepare for action with IFGOC • Use empathy and other interpersonal skills • Develop a mutually agreed-on focus of work and desired outcomes
Assessment	• Collect, organize, and interpret client data • Assess client strengths and limitations • Develop mutually agreed-on intervention goals and objectives • Select appropriate intervention strategies
Intervention	• Initiate actions to achieve organizational goals • Implement prevention interventions that enhance client capacities • Help clients resolve problems • Negotiate, mediate, and advocate for clients • Facilitate transitions and endings
Evaluation	• Critically analyze, monitor, and evaluate interventions

CHAPTER EXERCISES

1. Identify and describe the planned change process.

2. When is it appropriate for a social worker to terminate work with a client?

3. Identify the difference between verbal and nonverbal communication.

REFERENCES

Dolgoff, R., Feldstein, D., & Skolnik L. (1993). *Understanding social welfare (3rd ed.)*. New York, NY: Longman.

Healy, K. (2005). *Social work theories in Context: A Critical Introduction*. Hampshire: Palgrave MacMillan.

Richmond, M. (1922). *What is social case work?* New York, NY: Russell Sage Foundation

9

WORKING WITH GROUPS AND COMMUNITIES

LEARNING OBJECTIVES

This chapter focuses on examining practicing social work with groups. After reading this chapter, the reader will be able to

- identify the roots of social work practice with groups, and
- identity specific skills used in working with groups.

DEFINITION OF SOCIAL WORK GROUP WORK

As has been stated throughout this textbook, the social work profession is the professional activity of aiding individuals, groups, or communities in restoring or enhancing their capacity for social functioning and to create favorable societal conditions for achieving these goals. In the previous chapter, you learned about working with individuals (Chapter 8); this chapter focuses on mezzo practice, working with groups. Social work with groups represents a broad domain of direct social work and occurs in all settings in which social work is practiced. Humanistic values guide social work group work and guide the worker's role and use of self within the membership in a group.

HISTORY OF SOCIAL WORK PRACTICE WITH GROUPS

The roots of group social work began in the settlement houses, The Young Men's Christian Association (YMCA) and The Young Women's Christian Association (YWCA), Boy Scouts & Girl Scouts, & Jewish centers of the 1800s.   Social group work approaches are rooted in the group activities of various social agencies that began in the later part of the 19th century. Before the start of social work as a profession, services were provided by various community-based and faith-based individuals and groups. In the 20th century, group social worker and caseworker relationships were strained due to their different perspectives on the origin of the problems with their client bases. In addition, a great deal of misunderstanding existed concerning their roles and particularly the role of group work. Social work practice with groups advocated social change, whereas case workers viewed the profession more in terms of individual change.

Individual caseworkers had the perspective of blaming the victim and wanted to inquire what was wrong with the individual, which stemmed from the moral model of treatment. Early group workers recognized that social conditions such as the unequal distribution of wealth and the industrial revolution were the cause of the social problems people were experiencing. In contrast, case workers identified pathology as resting within the individual.

Social group work was presented to the profession at the National Conference for Social Work in 1935. At this conference, the concept and applicability of social group work was introduced as a process and technique that focused on the development and social adjustment of an individual through a group association. The need for group work gained recognition due in part, to the economic despair and psychosocial needs during the Great Depression. Social upheaval and new found demands as a result of post-Civil War industrialization, migration and immigration created many individual and societal needs. Some of these needs were met through group work endeavors found in settlement houses, religious, and charity organizations.

WORKING WITH GROUPS

Social work practice with groups builds on the essential element of human beings needing supportive relationships to build and grow (*Association for the Advancement of Social Work with Group, Inc. 2004*). Group work is the method of working with clients in groups for growth, the enrichment of social functioning, and for achieving desirable goals. Group work is a method of reducing or eliminating roadblocks to social interaction with the aim of accomplishing socially desirable purposes. Each individual within the group is a focus of concern and the group is the vehicle of growth and change. The enhancement of social functioning through the use of groups is the main goal of group work practice.

CULTURAL COMPETENCE AND WORKING WITH GROUPS

Working with diverse groups requires social workers to

- define key terms related to diversity;
- understand stereotyping and multiculturalism;
- identify their own stereotypes and preconceptions;
- possess in-depth knowledge of the diverse groups;
- work effectively with LBGTIQQ population in groups;
- apply the concepts of ethnicity-sensitive practice, empowerment, and the strength perspective;
- engage in culturally sensitive practice; and
- apply principles of feminist intervention in social work practice.

TYPES OF GROUPS

THERAPY GROUPS

Group therapy group aims to assist group members discover their feelings, thoughts, and behaviors for the purpose of lasting change. These groups can be either short term or long term and typically have the group members work on a particular problem, such as relationships, depression, anxiety disorders, or domestic violence to name a few. Cognitive behavioral therapy groups are one of the most popular types of therapy groups where the aim is changing the perspective of the presenting problem and developing healthy changes or coping mechanisms.

PSYCHOEDUCATIONAL GROUPS

The purpose of psychoeducational groups is to use information and educational processes to facilitate individual growth. Group therapy is a specific type of therapy that focuses on educating clients about their disorders and ways of coping, based on the principles of cognitive behavioral therapy.

SELF-HELP GROUPS

Self-help groups are not led by professionals, but rather, are led by members of the group. Twelve-step programs, such as Alcoholics Anonymous, are the most popular self-help groups. These groups encourage peer support both within and outside the group setting to help members recover from their problems. While social workers are not directly involved in running these groups, they can frequently provide guidance, and they work with clients who are members of many of these groups.

ONLINE SELF-HELP GROUPS

Sometimes due to mobility or lack of access to social workers or groups, online self-help groups can serve as a mechanism of connecting people with others through email, chat rooms, bulletin boards, and listservs. Four primary types of online self-help support networks are:

- email: writing messages to specific people,
- chat rooms: virtual spaces open during specified times for communication,
- bulletin boards: online resources usually open 24 hours a day for postings or communication, and
- listservs: allow large groups of people to send and receive information at any time.

Advantages of online self-help groups: (a) Provide services to homebound people for whom transportation to the offices of professionals is a major challenge, and (b) It is a good way to introduce people to seeking help. Disadvantages: (a) Lacks clear and accountable leadership, and (b) Members can have anonymity and not be held accountable for their comments.

EDUCATIONAL GROUPS

The purpose of educational groups is for group members to learn new, specific information. A social worker leading an education group could include ESL classes, job interviewing, or information on how to fill out job applications.

TASK GROUPS

Task groups are groups of individuals brought together to accomplish a specific action or produce a product. Task groups are groups in which specific work functions are accomplished. Five areas that are frequently cited by the experts on task groups are the five C's: Control, Conflict, Communication, Consensus, and Cohesion. The five C's can make or break a task group experience.

SUPPORT GROUPS

The aim of support groups is to assist otherwise healthy human beings with difficult life situations. In a support group, individuals can benefit from support, caring, and mutual aid. An example of a support group is a group for parents who have lost their children to a chronic illness.

YALOM'S THERAPEUTIC FACTORS

Yalom's (2005) therapeutic factors and model are possibly the most commonly applied principles to group work. Yalom's principles provide the social worker with a guide for practice and
a tool for periodic assessment. The social worker assesses whether each therapeutic factor is
present in the group and how it is impacting each client and the group as a whole.

INSTILLING HOPE

Social workers frequently meet clients at their emotional and physical low, and sometimes
clients have a sense of hopelessness. Groups should help members feel hopeful. Hope and
the expectancy of change are powerful therapeutic factors. It is believed that the power of
hope can help people be positive and aid in the change process.

UNIVERSALITY

Universality, the idea of "it can happen to us all" is important for the individual client and
for the group as a whole. Many clients believe that they are the only ones encountering this
problem, but being part of a group of people with similar experiences helps people see
that what they are going through is universal. Helping group members share their common
problems and concerns not only helps individuals, but it is also an important step in creating
group cohesion and goodwill.

IMPARTING INFORMATION

Group members can help each other by sharing information. Group members' exchange of
good information can lead to significant change and assist those giving information attain a
sense of purpose.

ALTRUISM

Being helpful and empathetic to others provide a sense of purpose and healing not only
for the individual receiving aid, but also for the person providing it. Group members often
report that helping others allows them to heal from their own problems. Group members who
provide support to others will feel more connected to the group, and typically less isolated.

THE CORRECTIVE RECAPITULATION OF THE FAMILY EXPERIENCE

Individual clients bring negative messages they receive from their families about themselves and others to the group setting. Yalom theorizes that the group becomes the context through which members can heal the painful experiences they had with their families. A group goal is for group members to learn that they are worthy of love.

DEVELOPMENT OF SOCIALIZING TECHNIQUES

Here, individual group members can develop healthy social skills by participating in training and role-playing within the group. Group members are then also encouraged to practice these new skills outside of the group.

IMITATIVE BEHAVIOR

The source of imitative behavior is based on social learning theory. The aim for the group leader is to model and shape behavior. Social workers can model desired behaviors and validate the behaviors they observe in group members that are congruent with healthy group dynamics.

INTERPERSONAL LEARNING

Individual group members participate in a process of relearning their values, roles, and needs with respect to others in their own lives. Learning new social skills and developing new methods of meeting their needs in the context of their relationships with others is a key goal here. Within this setting, group leaders encourage clients to experiment within and outside the group, and provide feedback regarding these newfound skills.

GROUP COHESIVENESS

Group cohesion is a feeling members feel about being part of the group. A cohesive group is almost like a healthy family, in that there is recognition that even when problems exist, members need to be there for one another. Social workers build group cohesion by validating supportive behavior, and being warm and being clear about the importance of group members supporting each other.

CATHARSIS

Catharsis, the release of intense emotions, is typically a powerful experience when it occurs in a group setting. When catharsis occurs for a group member, the group leader should model acceptance and focus on ensuring group members react without judgment, and without trying to instantaneously save the person from his or her intense emotional expression.

EXISTENTIAL FACTORS

Existential factors help group members realize that they are responsible for their own lives, actions, and choices; life and death are realities.

Member's commitment to a group goal will depend on:
- how attracted this member is to the group,
- how attractive the goal appears,
- how likely it appears the group can accomplish the goal,
- the ability to measure progress toward achieving the goal and the ability to measure when the goal is attained, and
- the rewards the group and the member will receive when the goal is attained.

Groups have a better chance to be effective when the following conditions are met:
- The goals are clear, operationally defined and measurable.
- The member sees the goals as being relevant, attainable, meaningful and acceptable.
- Both personal and group goals can be attained by the same activities and tasks.
- The goals are viewed as challenging and have a moderate risk of future reoccurence.
- The resources needed to accomplish the tasks are available.
- There is high coordination among group members.
- The group members maintain a cooperative, rather than a competitive atmosphere.

GROUP NORMS

Group norms: Every group develops its own habits and patterns for how to do things, which influence how the group is run and how group members communicate with each other. Norms can aid or impede groups in achieving their goals.
- A norm rule must be accepted by a majority of the group.
- Norms provide social control over members of groups.
- Norms can be established formally or informally.

Fig 9.1

Key Factors in Group Work

Clarity of purpose for leader and members:	A key factor for group leaders to be clear about the purpose of the group, which involves providing members with a sense of the purpose of each activity or group session.
Relevance of purpose to members:	Prescreening is a key and essential factor when group leaders are determining if the stated purpose of the group will be relevant to the needs and strengths of each group members.
Size of group:	The size of a group is significant and depends on the type of group, the group members, and the purpose of the group. For example, therapy, support, and growth groups should be small (6–10 members for adults, 4–6 members total for children), in order to support intensive discussion and dialogue. Educational and psychoeducational groups may be larger. Task groups can vary greatly in size, but are typically divided into sub-groups or broken into dyads and triads
Length of each session:	Length of group sessions is also an important factor in the success of a group. For instance, an hour and half of a behavioral modification group with kids diagnosed with ADHD boys is guaranteed to fail. This group would be successful if it were thirty minutes in length.
Frequency of meetings:	Groups typically meet once a week. Though of course there are exceptions to this rule, for example, intensive programs such as inpatient treatment facilities for substance abuse or for persons suffering from acute psychiatric episodes frequently have daily group therapy meetings.
Adequacy of setting:	The place of where the meetings are held must be conducive for counseling. For example, privacy is very important, a room large enough within a safe setting is essential.
Leader's attitude:	Leaders often undervalue the impact of their own behavior on the group process. Group members pick up clues about the leader's feelings toward groups and toward individual members. For the group leader, self-reflection is necessary so one understands how their behavior is impacting the group.
Members' level of commitment:	Group leaders must work to ensure that members are committed to the life of the group. They can do this by helping group members view the group as potentially supportive as soon as possible.
Level of trust among members:	Trust exercises are utilized to assist in having group members develop trust among their group members; trust must be earned.
Leader's readiness and experience with groups:	If a social worker does not have experience running a particular group, ideally serving as co-facilitator is the best way to learn. Otherwise, researching typical group goals for a specific group can help the social worker's readiness for leading a group.

- There should be a penalty in place for violating an important norm, determined by the group members.
- Some group norms are universal.
- Most norms are learned through positive and negative reinforcement.
- Some norms are established less formally by nonverbal communications (e.g., a head nod indicating something is wrong).
- Some norms become recognized only after they are violated.
- The goal of norms is to improve the function of the group.
- If norms are not enforced, they begin to lose their effectiveness.
- Group leaders ought to model the norms they believe are important.

Guidelines for Forming and Leading a Group

- Do your homework and plan ahead.
- Keep goals in mind when planning sessions.
- Relax before the start of a meeting.
- Pay attention to cues upon entering the meeting room.
- Seating arrangements are important.
- Make introductions and clarify roles.
- Provide an agenda ahead of time.
- Make additional guidelines as needed.

STAGES OF GROUP PROCESS

BEGINNING

Group social workers set the stage and take time to identify the purpose, clearly commit to the group's goals and procedures, and set expectations (Marmarosh, Holtz, & Schottenbauer, 2005). This stage is characterized as a time to convene, organize, and set a plan. Members are likely to remain distant or removed until they have had time to develop relationships.

- Intake: Present concerns and identify needs of prospective members. Determine if each individual can benefit from a group approach. Make tentative group goals. This is also referred to as a *contract stage*.
- Selection of members: Factors that create *homogeneity* or foster diversity within the group (i.e., age, sex, and level of education).
- Assessment and planning: A more in-depth assessment, and statement of goals, and plans for action occur during this stage.

MIDDLE

Almost all of the group's work occurs during this stage. Relationships are strengthened within the group to work on tasks. Problem solving is a term often used to describe this stage. Group leaders are usually less involved, but may remind the group of goals and rules and confront relationships that may be interfering with the overall purpose of the group.

END

This stage is marked by the accomplishment of the goals of the group, production of results, and the evaluation of the group's work. Preparation for termination should begin with the first session. The social worker helps members deal with feelings associated with termination of the group.

Evaluation and Termination: The decision to terminate a group is guided by the accomplishment of group or individual goals, expiration of a predetermined period of time, failure of the group to achieve desired ends, the relocation of the leader, or a shortage of funds.

CHAPTER EXERCISES

1. Identify 3 aspects of Yalom's therapeutic factors.

2. Discuss how the size of a group can impact the group process.

3. Identify the difference between an educational group and a task group; discuss when each group is appropriate.

REFERENCES

Association for the Advancement of Social Work with Groups. (2004). *Standards for social work practice with groups.* Retrieved from http://www.aaswg.org

Marmarosh, C., Holtz, A., & Schottenbauer, M. (2005). Group cohesiveness, group self-esteem, group-derived hope, and the well-being of group therapy members. *Group Dynamics: Theory, Research and Practice, 9*(1), 32–44.

Yalom, I.D. (2005). *The theory and practice of group psychotherapy: 5th Edition.* New York, NY: Basic Books.

10 SOCIAL WORK PRACTICE WITH ORGANIZATIONS AND COMMUNITIES

LEARNING OBJECTIVES

This chapter focuses on social work practice with organizations and communities. Social work with communities is a part of a generalist approach. After reading this chapter, the reader will be able to

- describe social work practice with communities and organizations, and
- analyze the planned changed process within the phases of social work community level interventions.

COMMUNITY SOCIAL WORKERS

- The aim of community organization is to stimulate and assist the local community to evaluate, plan, and coordinate efforts to provide for the community's health, welfare, and recreation needs.
- Community organizing is apt to include encouraging and fostering citizen participation, coordinating efforts between agencies or groups, public relations and public education, research, planning, and resource management.
- Community organizers act as catalysts for stimulating and encouraging community action.

Typically students interested in the social work profession are taught to conceptualize social problems and their solutions on a continuum from "micro" practice with individuals, to "mezzo" practice with families and groups to "macro" practice, which interacts with institutions, communities, and society at-large.

Though individual work or group works are more common areas of practice, many are also involved in community work, perhaps without realizing it. Other social workers' passion is community work and practice with organizations. Community social work practice based on a *capacity enhancement model* offers tremendous potential to unify communities consisting of groups from very different cultural backgrounds, and in the process of doing so make physical changes in the community. All social workers are ethically and professionally obligated to advocate for social work practice according to the National Association of Social Workers (NASW) *Code of Ethics* (2008); three of the six ethical principles emphasize this responsibility:

- Promote social change with and on the behalf of oppressed and vulnerable individuals and groups, with respect to poverty, unemployment, discrimination, and other areas of social and economic injustice.
- Address the needs of individuals, families, groups and communities.
- Practice with integrity within organizations in the areas of
  - social welfare,
  - influencing polices,
  - being active in emergencies (local and national), and
  - continuous work toward equity in access to resources.

HISTORY OF COMMUNITY PRACTICE IN SOCIAL WORK

The social work profession has been divided between a focus on the individual versus a focus on the community since the beginning of the profession, with two competing modes of ideologies: the Charity Organizations Society (COS) and the settlement house movement. COS aimed their attention entirely on individuals and aimed to offer charity and services to the deserving poor; within this model, the workers of the COS viewed their role as the "expert" in the process of change. Whereas, with respect to the settlement house movement, focus was on the environment and communities in which the poor lived. Workers in the COS believed that to truly understand their clients and the environment they had to move into the immigrant and oppressed areas and develop an understanding of the issues leading to an individual's poverty. Settlement house workers worked in collaboration with the poor to accomplish community change; here the role of the worker was one of a facilitator in the process of change. The rationale for emphasis on community level change in social work is the recognition that the problems people face are social, not individual. If the problem is ultimately one of injustice, then the solution is participatory change and revolution, not individual therapy or charity.

COMMUNITY CHANGE

The Civil Rights movement is a great example of how the power of solidarity can empower individual people and society to change. Such collective action is important because there was an understanding that their individual problems have social causes and joint solutions.

Community Development focuses on common presenting problems of oppressed populations and involvement in the process of overcoming externally imposed social problems. The job of the social worker in a Community Development framework lands heavily on the facilitator role. Community level practice promotes a quality of life, human rights, advocacy for human social and economic development, service program planning, social action, and social justice.

Many professionals in the social work field realize that communities are the hubs of societies where change needs to occur. Each community has their own distinct qualities that make it unique due to the emotional environments, physical environments, social, and psychological factors that impact individuals in a community. The definition of a community is a group of individuals (families and groups) that share one or more the following characteristics: values, geographic proximity, traditions, or institutions. Community social workers assist communities to function in a healthy manner. Some social workers work with individuals and conduct needs assessments and make referrals to resources in the community. Other duties include assessing needs on a larger scale, and planning and administering programs. One type of community social work practice is community organization. Social workers may be community builders or community organizers. They may be employed by various nonprofits and grassroots organizations to raise funds, write grants, gain support, and plan infrastructure.

COMMUNITY ORGANIZATION

Community organization is a type of community social work practice. The definition of an organization is a structured group of individuals that come together to achieve agreed upon objectives and goals.

Social workers not only help people with immediate needs, but also set up systems that will endure after they leave; this type of work also occurs on an international level. Many social workers want to pursue international work and have a desire to take their domestic experience abroad. The skills and qualities needed to be a successful domestic social worker are applicable in an international setting and can be particularly valuable for nonprofit and humanitarian organizations.

Fig 10.1

Models of Community Change

Social Planning Model	Experts design programs for communities and provide leadership. Involves problem solving to identify the specific needs of the community. Here, there is a top-down approach where the community member does not have a real voice in this process.
Social Action Model	With this model there is recognition of marginalized populations needing to organize in order to gain power for change. It brings awareness to the existence of social and economic injustice to community members. Community members organize themselves to redress imbalances in power, distribution/access of resources.
Locality Development Model	This model of community practice is based on the belief that in order to effect change, a wide variety of community people should be involved in planning, implementation, and evaluation. It involves a bottom-up approach where there is an emphasis of self-help and those in need giving direction to the change process. Self-help through mobilization of local resources.
Community Mobilization	Programs are externally designed, but community members are expected to contribute resources.
Community Action (A Conflict Perspective)	This approach redresses imbalances of power, resource allocation within a community.
Concerns Empowerment	This model of community change acknowledges that empowerment is something people do for themselves.
A Power-Coercive Approach to Change	Change agent as organizer helps the community identify pressure points. Media advocacy plays a role in getting the attention of decision makers.

Community change can build on the strengths of indigenous community-based organizations (CBOs), recognizing that such organizations are already engaged in the development and maintenance of the community. Strategies include community organization and advocacy based on social learning and community capacity theories. The community is the context for individual change. Using existing organizations, social networks, and communication channels to promote specific/targeted behavior changes of individual community members is essential.

PLANNED CHANGE PROCESS FOR SOCIAL WORK COMMUNITY PRACTICE

SENSING, ENGAGEMENT, AND RELATIONSHIP BUILDING

The first stage of the planned change process for community practice involves listening. Here the aim is to determine people's self-interest while observing the community. Typically, social workers do not live in the community, so they must introduce themselves in a manner that is not arrogant or with a wanting to fix the world attitude, but rather wanting to assist in bringing a positive change to the community. Here, establishing rapport, creating an atmosphere of mutual trust and respect, brainstorming with people and groups, identifying leaders, discovering politics, and clarifying ground rules and roles are all important factors to address. It is essential to learn about past efforts in an attempt to recognize those who may have been part of that effort, and understand why it failed so the same mistakes do not occur while formulating a strategy.

This is the "planning to plan" or developing an action framework stage. This stage identifies the community groups, organizations, and individuals involved, the funds available, political realities, and time needed for change. This stage is valuable because it explores the needs, resources, solutions, and individuals that must play a role in the solution, i.e., stakeholders.

CLARIFYING EXPECTATIONS, VISIONING, AND SETTING OVERALL DIRECTION

This stage postulates the overall framework and intentions of the change process by identifying areas of distress and creating vision statements. By setting the direction, the environment, parameters, purpose, and values for change are recognized. This stage also provides a sense of direction for those involved.

ASSESSING TO DISCOVER CAPACITIES, NEEDS, AND BARRIERS

Assessments involve gathering pertinent information. For this stage, the social worker must determine which data to collect, the source of the data, the methods of data collection, the analysis methods for the data, and the interpretation of the data into needs and capacities.

One way to determine what to assess is to examine the vision statement and guiding principles of the community (CSWE) (2008).

Analyzing a community involves examining

- community members,
- economic characteristics,
- community values,
- needs and social problems,
- oppression and discrimination,
- power structure,
- human services, and
- educational services.

The gathering of data and evidence (usually of five types of evidence) involves

- demographic information like age, race, socio-economic status, etc.;
- existing services attempting to address the needs of the community;
- identifying needs of the community stated by its members;
- identifying capacities for change, including resources and opportunities; and
- identifying barriers that block the use of existing resources or future solutions.

PRIORITIZING NEEDS

As with most communities, it is rarely the case that there are sufficient resources to address all of the identified needs. Once need statements are developed, prioritizing these needs is necessary to determine which should be addressed and in what order. Capacities can also be prioritized. This stage can be a very simple process or involve a lot of political maneuvering. Stakeholders often disagree over which problems get the most resources and which agency will contribute to the focus of change. The result of this stage should be a prioritized list of need statements, capacity statements, or both.

INTERVENTION PLANNING (SETTING GOALS AND OBJECTIVES)

This stage involves developing objectives and goals to postulate the solution, the implementation process, and the expected consequences. Goals are specific statements of the expected future outcomes. Objectives follow a SMART model: specific, measurable, attainable, and timely.

DEVELOPING IMMEDIATE ACTIVITIES AND RECOMMENDATIONS

Several alternative strategies to achieve the goals and objectives should be compared based on capacities, feasibility, cost-benefit, political realities, time constraints, and other considerations.

IMPLEMENTING

This stage carries out the goals and objectives using recommended action strategies. Implementation may be done by the person designing the change or contracted out to others.

FEEDBACK, MONITORING, AND EVALUATING

Feedback, monitoring, and evaluation are required to insure implementation progresses as intended and produces the anticipated results. Feedback is a process of periodically manually or automatically monitoring and reporting progress back to those who need it to change direction if necessary.

Feedback systems in organizations are often referred to as quality assurance or improvement programs. Monitoring is a continuous process to determine whether the process objectives are being carried out as intended. Evaluation is a periodic process to determine whether the outcomes stated in the "as measured by ..." part of the outcome objectives are being achieved and whether the outcomes relate to goal achievement.

TERMINATION

In this step, you determine if the goals are met, if the client is stable enough and has the support systems to continue without intervention, and if a referral to another service is needed. At some point in time, the social worker re-contacts the client to see if the results achieved were lasting or if the intervention cycle needs to be repeated.

CHAPTER EXERCISES

1. Identify three models of community change.
2. Identify eight factors for analyzing a community.
3. Discuss the history of community practice in social work.

REFERENCES

National Association of Social Workers. (2014). *NASW professional social work Code of Ethics.* Washington, DC: National Association of Social Workers.

Council on Social Work Education. (2008). *Educational policy and accreditation standards.* Retrieved from http://www.cswe.org/Accreditation/2008EPASDescription.aspx

11

SOCIAL WORK PRACTICE WITH OLDER ADULTS AND WITH CHILDREN AND FAMILIES

LEARNING OBJECTIVES

This chapter focuses on examining two main areas of social work fields of practice: working with older adults and working with children, adolescents, or both. After reading this chapter, the reader will be able to

- identify different practice settings where social workers are employed to work with older adults,
- identify different opportunities for fields of practice for social workers who work with children, and
- classify and identify the different roles of social workers with respect to these two different populations.

GERONTOLOGICAL SOCIAL WORKERS

Globally, the population is aging rapidly. Between 2015 and 2050, the proportion of the world's population over 60 years of age will nearly double, from 12% to 22% according to the World Health Organization (2015). In the United States, as baby boomers approach their sunset years, the population of the elderly will increase dramatically. By 2030, one out of five Americans will be over the age of 65. In 2011, the first baby boomers turned 65 years old. By 2029, all boomers will be at least 65. This cohort, an estimated 70 million people, will have a substantial impact on the U.S. health care system. The baby boom population, along with an increase in life expectancy, results in older adults making up a greater percentage of the U.S. population than ever. It is estimated the country will need 70,000 social workers that specialize in aging by 2020.

Mental health and emotional well-being are as important in older adults as in younger people. Approximately 15% of adults aged 60 and over suffer from a mental disorder, hence it is essential for social workers to understand and address the specific needs of older adults. High-quality care for older adults, many of whom have multiple complex chronic conditions, requires a diverse range of skills to address their physical, mental, cognitive, and behavioral needs. Today's older adults receive a high volume of health care services in many settings. Adults over 65 account for nearly 26% of all physician visits, 47% of all hospital stays, 34% of all prescriptions, 34% of all physical therapy patients, and 90% of all nursing home stays.

THE NEED FOR GERIATRIC SOCIAL WORKERS

The United States current health care system is overwhelmed by the need for geriatric care due to a lack of social workers specializing in the care of older adults. There is a great need for an increase in social work gerontologists since the projected need is so great. Approximately 55,000 social workers are needed in long-term care. By 2050, this number will double to approximately 109,000 (DHHS, 2006). Although nearly 75% of licensed social workers work with older adults in some capacity, many of them have not received education or training in gerontology (NASW, 2006). In 2009–2010, only 2.8% of BSW graduates and 6.7% of MSW graduates completed a specialization in aging (CSWE, 2011b).

Social workers who work with older adults are referred to as *gerontological* social workers; these professionals are trained in addressing the biopsychosocial needs of individuals 65 years or older. Social workers as well as other helping professions, recognize that older adults have characteristics distinct from other populations. One of the primary goals of the social worker is to acknowledge and address the specific challenges of this population by promoting independence, dignity, and autonomy. Those working in this realm of gerontology must be knowledgeable about social programs, policies, and legislation that affect older adults. The student will gain knowledge of the physical and psychological aspects of the aging process, of the needs and conditions of the elderly, and of the complex network of legislation and programs serving this population. Issues of bereavement, loss, loss of independence, and preparation for death are central to work in this field.

Social workers play a significant role in assisting family caregivers of older adults navigate through health and mental health networks, according to the NASW Standards for Social Work Practice with Family Caregivers of Older Adults. It notes that social workers are well-positioned to help older adults by using a strengths-based, person-in-environment approach.

Gerontological social workers may begin their work in the field by attaining either a bachelor's or master's degree. The skills needed to work with this population include: assessment, counseling, planning, discharge planning, crisis intervention, advocacy, brokering, individual, family and group counseling, interdisciplinary collaboration, administration, community organization, and research. Home visiting is often utilized. A key role that the social worker in this field of practice plays is being a broker; linking the client, their family, or both with needed resources. The typical settings for social workers who work with older adults are counseling services, in-home services, senior centers, hospitals, hospice, case management within local departments of social services, and adult homes or nursing homes.

Gerontological social workers may need to assess clients' functional capacity. They have expertise in assessing the difference between normal and abnormal aging processes. Geriatric social workers often work as discharge planners, ensuring that community-based services are in place when seniors exit the hospital setting to less intensive care. Clinical social workers provide therapy to elderly adults who are experiencing anxiety, depression, or other mental health illnesses. However, the focus of geriatric social workers is not solely on loss of function; social workers also assist older adults who have very active lives.

ASSESSMENT

1. Conduct a biopsychosocial assessment, which for an older person, includes

    - biological factors, such as information regarding physical functioning (e.g., health, illness and functional ability);

    - psychological factors, such as coping capacities, affect, and indicators of the need for a mental status examination;

    - social factors, such as: social roles (e.g., transitions, losses), social functioning, social support, social skills, and financial status;

    - family factors;

    - cultural factors;

    - spiritual factors; and

    - factors in the social and physical environment that affect the physical and emotional health of older persons (i.e., understanding that the interplay of psychological, social, and physical functioning is heightened in older persons).

2. Recognize and identify family, agency, community, and societal factors that promote or inhibit the greatest possible independence.

3. Demonstrate awareness of sensory, language, and cognitive strengths and limitations of clients.

4. Engage with older persons, utilizing their varying strengths.

5. Recognize indicators of the need for more in-depth assessment of areas of concern (e.g., substance abuse, elder abuse).

TREATMENT AND SERVICE CARE PLAN

- Set realistic and measurable objectives and establish care plans based on functional status, life goals, symptom management, and financial and social supports of older adults and their families.
- Reevaluate and adjust service/care plans for older adults to accommodate changes in their life circumstances.

CASE AND CARE MANAGEMENT

- Use social work case management skills to link elders and their families to resources and services.
- Collaborate with other social service, health, mental health, and allied health professionals in delivering services to older adults.
- Assess and leverage organizational and community resources in meeting needs of older adults and their caregivers.

INTERVENTIONS

- Engage older persons and family caregivers in maintaining and enhancing their mental and physical health and functioning.
- Assist older persons and their families in dealing with stressful or crisis situations.
- Enhance the coping capacities of older persons, including abilities to deal with loss and transition.
- Provide services to older persons and their families through group modalities.

CHILD, FAMILY, AND SCHOOL SOCIAL WORKERS

Child, family, and school social workers work with children and youth along with their parents and guardians. Approximately 16% of the country's half a million social workers work in child services; 12% work in family services. A range of factors including poverty, homelessness, alcohol and drug addiction, and child abuse and neglect make today's families more susceptible to needing social services. Less than half of the children that live in the United States have a traditional nuclear family. Some of the duties that social workers who work with this population do are listed below:

- Counsel families to find better coping strategies and solutions to their problems.
- Place abused children in loving homes.
- Help children and families make best use of the welfare system.
- Assist homeless families in finding housing.
- Help pregnant women, adoptive parents and adopted children navigate the adoption system.

Social workers working with children recognize that a significant part of the treatment approach must include the family. Strategies are examined to fully understand facts that affect the entire family unit, including parents, other children and legal guardians. Social workers consider methods that help improve clients' well-being and quality of life. A social worker working with children may counsel clients who have difficulty adjusting socially, have academic problems, or mental or physical health issues. Social workers also work with children who are in stable home environments, but may need help with other mental health issues such as behavioral issues, bullying, or making friends. Some social workers work in the public school system, typically in elementary or middle schools and may be assigned to one school or work at several schools splitting the days of the week. Other social workers work for governmental organizations, residential care facilities, adoption agencies, etc. Home visits are part of the job for many social workers who work with children and youth, since assessing the family and home environment is a key part of the process.

Social workers trained in the Children and Families concentration, work in a range of settings, such as

- schools,
- mental health clinics,
- juvenile courts,
- child protection agencies, and
- community-based organizations.

In all of the settings mentioned above, social workers use a systems and family-oriented approach to helping families cope. Students can pursue social work at the bachelor's or master's level. Bachelor's programs (BSW) prepare the generalist for casework and service delivery with individuals and families. Master's programs offer the student a specialization, like the children and families concentration, for example.

SCHOOL SOCIAL WORKER

School social work has a 100-year history. Social work was introduced to this setting in response to the awareness by school personnel that emotional factors often hinder learning for some students, making it hard to focus on academics. A majority of the duties include ensuring compulsory school attendance, exhibiting appropriate classroom behavior and adjustment to the classroom for the student. Addressing preventive interventions regarding developmental tasks and adjustments (socialization, substance abuse, teen suicide) is essential as a school social worker. Although some states will allow bachelor's level social workers to work in the schools, the majority requires master's degrees. The School Social Work Association of America link listed below is a great resource that summarizes the requirements to be a school social worker in a number of states (http://www.sswaa.org/). This link provides a wealth of information regarding if a particular state issues a school social work certificate, requires a social work license, or both. Social workers trained as school social workers work in a range of settings:

- school districts,
- alternative high schools,
- Boards of Cooperative Educational Services (BOCES) learning centers, and
- preschools.

Some of the duties of school social workers include assessment, crisis intervention, group work, individual work, preventive training, peer mediation, program development, grant writing, and program evaluation. Family involvement will vary from setting to setting. Social workers in the schools respond to crises in the classroom and assess and counsel school children who are experiencing stress, acting out, being targeted by bullies, or who are the bullies. Social workers also provide support and therapy to children who have experienced traumas, losses, or abuse. Some school social workers work on the Child Study team, alongside school psychologists and other professionals to assess whether students need additional academic or mental health support.

CHILD WELFARE

Social workers who specialize in child welfare seek to improve the well-being of children and youth and their families, with the goal of protecting or intervening on their client's behalf when a child is experiencing child maltreatment (physical, emotional or sexual abuse and/or neglect). Social workers who work in the child welfare system may advise in cases where parents cannot or will not protect or provide for their children, and concurrently work to find adoptive homes for children.

Child welfare as a field of social work practice has traditionally been concerned with the needs of children and their families when parental functioning is impaired or when the child is in need of social services due to developmental, emotional, or behavioral problems. The main focus in child welfare is on strengthening the family in order to keep the child with the family and prevent out of home placement or termination of parental rights. With the use of family preservation services and family supportive services, social workers serve an instrumental role in working to keep families together. Some of these interventions include helping to stabilize immediate crises, strengthening family relationships, and teaching parenting skills. In the arena, services provided are divided between social workers who provide services to children in their own homes and those professionals who provide services to children removed from their parents' care and are in placed in foster or kinship care.

Child welfare workers must be knowledgeable and be on top of any state policies regarding child protection services, since each state has their own laws. In this arena, social workers assess at risk families to determine if a child needs placement. They evaluate potential foster homes, monitor the foster home during placement, and help legal authorities and the family determine an appropriate time to return the child to the family of origin. Child welfare social workers work in a range of settings that include

- service for children in their own home;
- day care, adoption, group home care;
- foster family care;
- residential care.

Social workers use the following skills when working as a child welfare worker: assessment and treatment planning, crisis intervention, individual, family, and group work, advocacy, and collateral work with ancillary agencies. Program development, community organization, research, development of assessment tools, and development of training and educational programs are also needed skills in some settings.

FAMILY SERVICES

Family services are addressed directly to families and children. This area of social work has customarily had a more preventive focus than the field of child welfare. Goals focus on strengthening the family and keeping them intact. Services may include family counseling, anger management, parental skills or education, and addressing issues of personal and family growth and development. The typical settings where family services social workers are employed include family service agencies, YMCA, and neighborhood service and community centers. The social workers help any individual who is a family member—adults and children—in need of family supportive services (prevention); family service agencies are often contracted to serve clients from the protective service agencies and to provide counseling mandated by the court.

When working with this population, the social worker frequently works with families where abuse, mental illness, or physical illness plays a significant role in the presenting problem(s). Here, the social worker may aid parents by linking them to necessary resources so that the children can stay in the home or return home.

SOCIAL WORKERS WHO WORK WITH ADOLESCENTS

Services and programs intended to address the unique needs of adolescents are often geared to prevention and outreach interventions. Here the main emphasis is to help the adolescent recognize and attain their developmental potentials. These techniques often include educationally oriented recreation, and handicrafts and sports activities designed to aid the adolescent in being emotionally healthy while learning healthy coping strategies, social skills, and proper moral conduct. Although the focus is on the adolescent client, some programs will also work with their families and on strengthening the communication and behavioral problems that exist between them. Child welfare social workers work in a range of settings that include

- youth bureaus,
- school settings,
- YMCA, YM-YWHA,
- community or youth centers,
- emergency shelters,
- suicide prevention programs, and
- job training programs.

Typically, theories and intervention used when working with this population include: assessment, individual, family and group counseling, community organization and outreach, preventive education, suicide prevention, safe sex education, advocacy and research, crisis theory, and short and long term counseling.

CHAPTER EXERCISES

1. Identify different opportunities for fields of practice for social workers who work with children.

2. Identify different practice settings where social workers are employed when working with older adults.

3. Classify and identify the different roles social workers function in with respect to these two different populations.

REFERENCES

Council on Social Work Education. (2011). *Why recruit students to gerontological social work?* Retrieved from http://www.cswe.org/File.aspx?id=31797

Council on Social Work Education. (2011). *2009 Statistics on social work education in the United States.* Retrieved from http://www.cswe.org/CentersInitiatives/DataStatistics/ProgramData/47673.aspx

National Association of Social Workers. (2006a). *Assuring the sufficiency of a frontline workforce: A national study of licensed social workers—Special report: Social work services for older adults.* Retrieved from: http://workforce.socialworkers.org/studies/aging/aging.pdf

U.S. Department of Health and Human Services. (2006). *The supply and demand of professional social workers providing long-term care services. Report to Congress.* Retrieved from http://aspe.hhs.gov/daltcp/reports/2006/SWsupply.htm

World Health Organization. (2015). Ageing and health factsheet No. 404. Retrieved from http://www.who.int/mediacentre/factsheets/fs404/en/

PROVIDING SOCIAL WORK SERVICES IN A VARIETY OF SETTINGS WITH DIFFERENT POPULATIONS

12

LEARNING OBJECTIVES

This chapter focuses on the social work profession and working with different populations. After reading this chapter, the reader will be able to

- identify key features of working with different populations; and
- examine different settings where social workers are employed.

MENTAL HEALTH AND SOCIAL WORK

Mental health is comprised of the psychological, emotional, and social well-being of individuals. One's mental health affects how one feels, thinks, and acts. It also helps determine how one handles stress, makes life choices, and relates to others. Mental health is important in each phase of life, from childhood, to adolescence, to adulthood.

Many factors contribute to mental health problems, including

- biological factors, i.e., genes or brain chemistry;
- life experiences that include, but are not limited to, trauma or abuse; and
- family history of mental health problems.

Medical conditions affect far more than the body. They can result in an onslaught of emotional, financial, and social needs. Social workers are adept at helping people meet these sorts of needs, and so we find social workers in many locations where health services are delivered. They are known as medical and health care social workers. They may serve as case managers, patient navigators, and therapists.

Mental health social workers work with clients who have mental illness, such as depression, schizophrenia, complex sets of comorbid conditions, bipolar disorder, and personality disorders, to name a few diagnoses. Social workers with a master's degree (MSW) can provide psychotherapy. They also provide case management services for individuals with complex needs. In hospital settings, social workers plan discharges and assist in navigating systems so that the individual has the resources and support needed when leaving the hospital.

In mental health settings, a variety of professionals from different disciplines are employed to meet the client's needs. The social worker serves as part of the treatment team, which also includes a psychologist and a psychiatrist. In this capacity, the social worker provides counseling to the client as well as acts as a broker to ensure and make linkages to other services needed to meet treatment goals. The social worker also handles the client's discharge and adjustment to the community. Mental health clinic services include assessments, diagnoses, and treatment or counseling. These services are provided to assist an individual or group in alleviating mental or emotional illness, symptoms, conditions, or disorders. These services are intended to respond to a crisis that requires immediate attention, such as a suicide attempt or an acute psychotic episode. Individuals with emotional problems who can remain in the community and continue to function in other areas of their lives are offered out-patient services.

PSYCHIATRIC SOCIAL WORKERS

Psychiatric social workers provide mental health services to individuals with great needs. They conduct psychotherapy and diagnose mental illness. Social workers in inpatient settings often have the responsibility for pulling together the discharge plan. The goal is ambitious: that the person will have the resources to function optimally within the community. Due to managed care, now hospital stays are shorter than in the past. Therefore, it may be the case that the patient needs to transition to a residential care center or a day program. Psychiatric social work has progressed from in-patient treatment to include of an array of services in the community for prevention and provisions for aftercare.

Psychiatric hospitals provide treatment for individuals diagnosed with mental illnesses and provide mental health services in settings such as acute care, partial hospitalization, and residential care. Severe depression, psychotic episodes, severe anxiety, and substance-related disorders are some of the illnesses treated in a psychiatric hospital. Admission to a psychiatric ward can be on a voluntary basis, or patients are involuntarily committed in cases where the patients may pose a danger to themselves or others.

Clinical social workers offer therapy that focuses on behavior and cognitive modification and supportive psychotherapy. Social workers are respected members of the multidisciplinary treatment team, providing individual, group, and family therapy, and rehabilitation services. Social workers also conduct psychosocial assessments. They meet with other professionals that comprise the mental health team (psychiatrists, nurse practitioners, psychologists) to discuss patient care.

Psychiatric social workers may also be employed in outpatient centers, working with children, adolescents, or adult clients. In this setting, the social worker conducts psychotherapy and assessments, educates the patient and family members about their diagnosis and other presenting problems, and makes referrals when necessary. Furthermore, social workers serve as case managers for clients who require periodic hospitalization, intensive use of community resources, or both.

HEALTH AND MEDICAL SOCIAL WORKERS

Social work practiced in the health field has its main focus on advocacy and serving as a broker for services concerning the biopsychosocial aspects of the client's and family's situation within the range of the continuum of health care. There is a particular emphasis on the unserved and underserved. The largest percentage of healthcare social workers work in a hospital setting, though some work in outpatient health centers. Typical settings where social workers can be employed include hospitals, health centers, public health agencies, community based health agencies, nursing homes, hospice care, and rehabilitation centers.

In hospital settings, social workers administer discharge planning and address any presenting problems that new admissions may have. The main aim of social workers in these settings is to help patients find resources within their communities. Social workers coordinate care for patients, who are expected to need a continuum of services during their stay and for aftercare. A hospital social worker may have a caseload of patients with widely varying needs of services, including finding insurance, assisting with aftercare, and dealing with medical concerns and diagnoses. Typically, patients need assistance in weighing the risks and benefits of different healthcare options. Advanced directives or making end of life planning is also a key feature of this setting. Depending on the education of the social worker, those employed in a medical setting sometimes treat or diagnose psychological conditions.

Social work clients in health care settings include individuals with acute and chronic illness. The range of clients served is often directed to vulnerable populations (the elderly, the economically challenged, those living in poverty, the homeless, and other underserved populations).

WORKING WITH CLIENTS IN THE MILITARY OR WHO ARE VETERANS

Military social work is a specific field of practice that delivers support and interventions to military personnel, their spouses and children, and retirees. This care for service members, veterans and their families focuses on dealing with a range of physical, mental and psychosocial issues.

Military social workers receive specialized training that allows them to serve the needs of military clients. Social workers have accompanied troops in virtually every deployment in recent times and are working with the families on the home front as well. Active military members, their families, and veterans must deal with challenges unique to military life. Military social workers play a vital part in connecting them to resources. These specialized social workers work with and support military personnel facing deployment, active duty, and transitioning back home. In addition, social workers work with veterans dealing with psychological and physical effects upon returning home. They also assist families who need emotional and financial support, as well as military-impacted schools and communities. With respect to families, young children may not truly understand why their parent is gone, which can make children act out. Children as well as family members fear that their loved one won't return. When the person does return, there is another adjustment process.

A key component of working with this population is collaborating with local agencies to identify and serve military populations in their communities. For returning service members, social workers must assist with health and employment services. Social workers working with military personnel offer services such as individual and family counseling, mental health therapy, and crisis intervention. In addition, social workers offer therapy and counseling to the whole family.

ASSISTING VETERANS

Military personal, transitioning back to civilian life and dealing with post-traumatic stress due to being injured in the line of duty, or unresolved grief, are among the major challenges faced by veterans. Social workers do not work solely on presenting issues related to service in the military, but rather, assist veterans with a variety of life issues. Military social work is not limited to direct practice. The social work profession also advocates on a macro level for instance, working to increase benefits. Social workers help veterans apply for benefits from the VA and other organizations.

PALLIATIVE AND HOSPICE SOCIAL WORKERS

Hospice and palliative care social workers work with individuals who are nearing the end of life and individuals who are living with chronic illnesses. Assistance and support to the client and their family include providing emotional, spiritual, and physical support so clients are as comfortable as possible physically. Social workers may act as navigators and care coordinators. Social workers help clients and families understand their options, identify services they need, and fill out the necessary paperwork. A crucial part of the paperwork is assisting with an advanced directive: a written statement of an individual's wishes regarding medical treatment, often including a living will. This document ensures those wishes are carried out should the individual be unable to communicate them to a doctor.

Palliative and hospice social workers lead support groups and offer in-service training to other professionals who are involved in the treatment. Pain management is also a key feature when working with this population; social workers may also teach clients non-pharmaceutical techniques for managing pain. Palliative care and hospice care are related, but not one and the same. Hospice care emphasizes relieving symptoms and supporting patients with a life expectancy of months to live. Palliative care may be provided at any time during a patient's illness, from the diagnosis and beyond. Palliative care is specialized medical care for people with serious illness and focuses on providing relief from the symptoms and stress. The goal is to improve quality of life for both the patient and their family. Some individuals transition from palliative care to hospice when they are in the final stages of an illness, but this is not the case for all. Not all who receive palliative care are near death.

CRIMINAL JUSTICE/CORRECTION

Social workers in the field of criminal justice can work in a variety of settings including juvenile and family courts, adult criminal court, probation, jails, and community based services and alternative sentencing programs. Social workers in the area of criminal justice are obliged by three core ethical and professional obligations: to improve the mental health needs of their clients, and to return individuals to the community who will be productive, and serve the interests of public safety. Social workers provide assessments, diagnoses, treatment, individual and group work, crisis intervention, and recommendations. Therapy to sex offenders, conflict mediation, or victim advocates are all potential roles in this arena.

A prime function for the social worker is to serve the court in assessment and sentencing, ensuring due process of the law, from the arrest to the trial to prison and release. Aspects of the social worker's role involve the assessment of granting parole, and recommendations for work release programs, pre-release guidance centers, and halfway houses. In addition, social workers also screen, evaluate, and treat law enforcement and other criminal justice personnel who need mental health services.

Important features of working in this area of social work include interdisciplinary collaboration, rehabilitation programs, community organizing, program development, and research. Some social workers serve as probation officers, case managers, or therapists for prisoners. Some serve as an expert witness. Social workers also write reports about defendants that contain evidence about the defendant's decision-making capabilities, medical health, and mental health. Functions of the social worker may include providing consultation, education or training to juveniles in the justice and correctional systems, law makers, law enforcement personnel, attorneys, law students, and paralegals. Other functions include but are not limited to policy and program development; mediation, advocacy, and arbitration; teaching, training, and supervision; and behavioral science research and analysis.

SOCIAL WORK PRACTICE IN CRIMINAL JUSTICE AND WORKING WITH MINORS

Social workers in the criminal justice system who work with children often become advocates for treating children with different legal standards, as compared to adults, according to the National Association of Social Workers (https://www.socialworkers.org/pressroom/features/issue/advocacy.asp). Another possible role deals with child custody issues or the necessity to appoint a guardian if a parent dies or becomes incapacitated. On the other side of the spectrum, juveniles who are in the criminal justice system due to committing a crime or are the victim of a crime may need the aid of a social worker to assist with the minor's ability to testify. Social workers may also have to assess the minor's ability to make medical decisions.

CHAPTER EXERCISES

1. List typical settings where mental health social workers can be employed.

2. Describe some of the unique challenges veterans face.

3. List two opportunities social workers have in the criminal justice field.

REFERENCES

Council on Social Work Education. (2011). *Why recruit students to gerontological social work*? Retrieved from http://www.cswe.org/File.aspx?id=31797

Council on Social Work Education. (2011). *2009 Statistics on social work education in the United States.* Retrieved from http://www.cswe.org/CentersInitiatives/DataStatistics/ProgramData/47673.aspx

National Association of Social Workers. (2016). *Practice and Professional Development.* Retrieved from https://www.socialworkers.org/practice/health/default.asp

National Association of Social Workers. (2012). *Service members, veterans, and their families.* Retrieved from https://www.socialworkers.org/practice/military/documents/MilitaryStandards2012.pdf

National Association of Social Workers. (2010). *Social workers in hospice and palliative care.* Retrieved from http://workforce.socialworkers.org/studies/profiles/Hospice.pdf

U.S. Department of Health and Human Services. (2006). *The supply and demand of professional social workers providing long-term care services. Report to Congress.* Retrieved from http://aspe.hhs.gov/daltcp/reports/2006/SWsupply.htm

Wilson, M. (2010). *Criminal justice social work in the United States: Adapting to new challenges.* Washington, DC: NASW Center for Workforce Studies.

13

SOCIAL WORK TODAY AND THE FUTURE OF THE PROFESSION

LEARNING OBJECTIVES

This chapter focuses on the social work profession today, and its future. After reading this chapter, the reader will be able to

- identify key features of the social work profession; and
- examine some changes for the future and how the profession will be impacted.

UNITED STATES DEMOGRAPHICS

In the social work profession we must be cognizant of the populations we serve, and the future outlook of the clients we will serve. One of the major tenets of the profession and the code of ethics is being culturally competent (as discussed in Chapter 2). We need to be prepared about what our clients will look like in terms of age, race and ethnicity, religion, family structure, socioeconomic levels, and the services these populations will need.

The United States population is 314 million and projections expect the population will increase to 420 million people by the year 2060. It has been estimated that the non-Hispanic White population will not be the majority, but rather the Hispanic population will be the majority in the United States (U.S. Census Bureau, 2012). As the United States becomes increasingly diverse, social workers' competence in serving diverse populations is critical. Without cultural awareness, social workers add to oppression when working with clients from other cultures.

There are specific skills to achieve cultural competence, such as learning and examining one's own beliefs, values, and culture, and determining to what extent clinical interventions are based in Eurocentric, Western, middle-class, and American values.

THE INCREASING AGING POPULATION

The older population, individuals 65 years or older, were 46.2 million in 2014, representing 14.5% of the U.S. population (one in every seven Americans). By 2060, projections indicate there will be about 98 million older persons, more than twice their number in 2014. The baby boomer generation, which comprises 27% of the U.S. population, started reaching the age of 70 in 2016 (U.S. Department of Health, 2014).

The increase in the aging population of the U.S. presents social, economic, and political implications for both the social work profession and the country as a whole. Social workers serve various roles with aging individuals and their families, including in community-based programs, health care settings, retirement and assisted living settings, nursing homes and other long-term care settings, and palliative and hospice care, and must be aware of the needs and changing needs of this population.

Over 4.5 million people age 65 and over (10%) were living below the poverty level in 2014. Over 2.5 million older adults were classified as "near-poor". Of course there are race disparities regarding the elderly and who is living in poverty: For White seniors, 2.8 million (7.8%) were poor in 2014, compared to 19.2% of African-Americans, 14.7% of older Asians, and 18% of older Hispanics who were identified as living in poverty.

When assessing clients, individually or with their families, workers need to explore ethnicity. Assessments should include the influence of culture and how the person's community can be helpful. The assessment should also include issues of birthplace, immigration experience, length of time in the country, and language. The *culturagram* (Congress, 2004) is an assessment guide for understanding immigrant populations. When providing interventions, social workers need to include empowerment as a goal.

The growth in the aging population impacts four areas of social welfare policy: 1) Social Security and Medicare social insurance benefits, 2) viability of the formal long-term care system, 3) adequacy of family resources, and 4) a scarce and competing pool of social welfare resources. There is an array of social welfare policy implications related to the trends discussed above, the most debated being the need to revise and revamp the financing and benefit structures of the Social Security and Medicare funds. The increase in the elderly population has enormous implications for social welfare policies because of the increase in the ratio of those that need entitlement claims compared to the taxes placed on the labor market earnings of the younger working-age generations.

THE CHANGING FAMILY DEMOGRAPHICS

The family unit is often one of the most influential and important parts of an individual's life. Families are the source of development for an individual's morals, values, and interpersonal skills. A family is a social institution that is found in every culture and has been defined as a group of people related by marriage, ancestry, or adoption that live together in a common household. The members that make up the family offer emotional and financial support for most individuals. Individuals who grow up in a dysfunctional family will often have family problems themselves as adults.

Family social workers provide services to families in crisis that need help fixing problems that interfere with family harmony. Families experiencing crises will need help picking up the pieces and rebuilding their lives. Typically, families need the services of a social worker due to having problems that they cannot mend or fix on their own. These problems often negatively impact the "normal" functioning of a healthy family and may include substance abuse, mental illnesses, medical problems, financial problems, work and family obligations, and other life stressors.

The significant diversity of families and family structures force social workers to re-think family treatment plans. A snapshot into the family composition in the United States indicates that approximately half of all families with children under age 18 are composed of nuclear families. So what does the other 50% of families look like? Twenty-seven percent of households with children under age 18 are made up of single-parent families. Approximately 670,000 families with children under age 18 have a family member age 65 or older living with them. Roughly 2.5 million children under age 18 live with one or both parents in their grandparents' home. About 20% of children in two-parent households live in blended families. An estimated 415,129 children were in foster care in 2014. Approximately 1.3 million children under age 18 live with their grandparents. Approximately 3% of children have parents who are gay, lesbian, or bisexual (DHHS, 2011). Social workers must learn from the client how the family composition impacts the client's presenting problems i.e., whether the family serves as a support system, or is negatively impacting the client. When working with children and families, the social worker must realize that their client's definition of family may not fit their own definition.

POVERTY

There are large variations in poverty rates according to age, sex, marital status, race, ethnicity, nativity, and geographic location. The households that are more likely to fall into poverty are female-headed, single-parent households. The poverty rate for family households headed by single female parents is three times more than that for two parent households and about twice the rate of single-parent households headed by males (U.S. Census Bureau, 2010). The fact that family composition is at risk for poverty because of the disadvantaged status of a single female parent suggests four basic social policy alternatives: reducing earnings disparities between men and women, increasing the income and in-kind subsidies to economically disadvantaged single-parent families, discouraging non-marital child bearing, and pursuing policies that might promote the formation and stability of two-parent households

In terms of race and ethnicity, the groups that share a disproportionate risk of living in poverty include American Indians and Alaska Natives (29.1%), African Americans (27.4%), and Hispanics (26.5%) (U.S. Census Bureau, 2013). African American households make 58% of the median income for non-Hispanic White households, Hispanic households 70%, and Asian households 118% of the median income of White households (DeNavas-Walt, Proctor, Smith, 2012).

In response to lack of equal access and opportunity in education, employment, housing, health and mental health care and services, social services, and criminal justice, among other areas, NASW advocates for an inclusive, multicultural society where age, ethnicity, race, class, sexual orientation, physical and mental ability, religion and spirituality, gender, and other social identities are respected. The organization's *Code of Ethics* includes the belief that social workers should challenge social and economic injustice regarding issues of poverty, unemployment, discrimination, and other manifestations, and that their activities should promote sensitivity to and knowledge of oppression and cultural and ethnic diversity. Furthermore, the *Code* states, social workers must work to safeguard access to needed information, services, and resources; equality of opportunity; and meaningful participation in decision-making for all individuals.

IMMIGRATION AND TRANSNATIONALISM

Immigrants make up a significant segment of U.S. society. Immigration to the United States has had a steady growth resulting in changes in ethnic composition. The challenge for social work is to advocate for the social service needs of immigrants by creating appropriate programs that will contribute to the social and economic integration of immigrants. Working toward fair immigration and refugee policies is central to the profession of social work and vital to the awareness of human rights. Social workers recognize migration as a multifaceted social, political, and cultural process.

Social workers create and organize community support programs for refugee families in the U.S. and internationally, and advocate for refugee resettlement services. In the U.S., social workers assist newly arrived refugees with resettlement. Internationally, social workers work with humanitarian aid organizations such as UNICEF, coordinate psychosocial programs for children in refugee camps, or work to effect policy and design programs.

It is essential for social workers to know the dynamics of migration as well as the implications of immigration policy on individuals and families in order to effectively support immigrants and refugees in the U.S. and internationally. Immigration and acculturation may be stressful and even traumatizing. Immigration often separates families from their extended family, resulting in an enormous loss of support. Upon arrival in the U.S., families must adapt to a different culture and become acculturated to American culture. We have all heard of people in the United States commenting on people not "looking or acting American". Have you ever asked yourself what does it mean to look or act American? For some, it's what we have been socialized to believe about what an American is. For people who migrate here, the process of "becoming American" can be a stressful one. Even when people have acculturated, they may never been viewed as American, due to their skin color, accent, religious affiliation, etc. Social workers need to understand this can serve as a stressor as well. Becoming acculturated is a process that involves changing one's cultural practices while learning a new culture and discarding parts of a previous culture.

Individuals' immigration and acculturation experiences vary based on country of origin and individual circumstances. Social workers must realize that everyone's immigration experience will be different due to the country of origin: did the individual arrive as a refugee due to political or religious persecution in the home country? In the U.S., practice and policy on local, state, national, and international levels must take into account relocation changes in the face of global realities.

The future of immigration: it is estimated that by 2060 the U.S. population is predicted to add another 120 million people and have the following ethnic composition: 25% Hispanic, 13% African American, 8% Asian, 4.8% non-Hispanic two or more races, and about 42% non-Hispanic White (U.S. Census Bureau, 2012).

MULTILINGUALISM

Multilingualism refers to the ability to speak more than one language (sign language is of course included in this definition). Social workers recognize that effective communication and use of language are crucial factors for culturally appropriate practice. Social workers must promote services through culturally appropriate language specifically written information. With the growing numbers of immigrants from Latin American countries, the Spanish language is a great asset to have as a social worker.

- As the U.S. population continues to become increasingly diverse, proficiency in multiple languages enables social workers to communicate more effectively with clients.
- Spanish follows English as the second most common language spoken in the United States, but there is a need for social workers fluent in other languages as well, including Russian, Chinese, and Arabic.

JOB OUTLOOK FOR THE SOCIAL WORK PROFESSION

Careers in the field of human services and social work are quite numerous and may include gerontology aide, child advocate, child abuse case worker, social work assistant, assistant case manager, life skills counselor, social services technician, drug abuse counselor, adult day care worker, mental health aide, crisis intervention counselor, therapeutic assistant, and even probation officer. The Bureau of Labor Statistics (2014) foresees that increased demand for healthcare and social services will bring employment growth of 19% for social workers in a variety of specialty areas. This growth will be driven by the needs of children and of the aging population, as well as substance abusers. Child and family social workers will be in demand to assist families with healthy parenting and preventing the occurrence of child maltreatment.

Due to the rising need for social services for youth and their families, the employment demand for child, family, and school social workers is expected to grow faster than average for all professions by 15% between 2012 and 2022. Employment will be available at all levels of state, local, and governmental facilities in programs that serve the elderly, socially displaced, mentally impaired, or developmentally disabled.

Due to the rising prevalence of individuals diagnosed with mental health disorders and drug addiction social workers will be in demand to work with these populations. Jobs for substance abuse and mental health social workers are projected to have an increase of 26,000 new jobs between 2012 and 2022.

THINGS FOR SOCIAL WORKERS TO ALWAYS CONSIDER AND WORK ON

As you consider this field of work as a profession, some things that should always be in the forefront of a professional's mind are the following goals:

- Analyze root causes of inequality and injustice.
- Emphasize power dynamics.
- Juxtapose goals of market economy and social work.
- Critique the role of ideology and culture.
- Focus on basic institutions and human needs.

CHAPTER EXERCISES

1. Identify the expected change in family composition and how this may impact family dynamics.

2. Identify the importance of cultural competence when social workers work with immigrants.

3. Describe the job outlook for the social work profession.

REFERENCES

Bureau of Labor Statistics. (2014). *Social workers*. In *Occupational Outlook handbook* (2014–2015 ed.). https://www.socialworkers.org/pressroom/features/issue/advocacy.aspthe

DeNavas-Walt, C., Proctor, B. D., and Smith, J. C. (2013). *Income, poverty, and health insurance coverage in the United States: 2012*. Retrieved from http://www.census.gov/prod/2013pubs/p60-245.pdf

U.S. Census Bureau. (2012, 2013). *New census bureau report analyzes U.S. population projections*. Retrieved from https://www.bls.gov/ooh/

U.S. Census Bureau. (2010). *Income, poverty, and health insurance coverage in the United States: 2010*. Retrieved from http://www.npc.umich.edu/poverty

U.S. Department of Health and Human Services. (2014). *Health disparities*. HealthyPeople.gov. Retrieved from http://www.healthypeople.gov/2020/about/disparitiesAbout.aspx

CPSIA information can be obtained
at www.ICGtesting.com
Printed in the USA
BVHW021931060423
661905BV00003B/51